H. M. Bateman

The Prion Cartoon Classics series, brings together anthologies of drawings from the top artists in the field working in Britain and around the world. Concentrating on simple joke cartoons, each volume is carefully selected in consultation with the artist's family and introduced by a renowned figure in the media. The collections — which often bring an artist's work together in a single volume for the very first time — also contain brief biographies of each cartoonist. This unique series will be welcomed both by those who have long sought out-of-print books by the greatest cartoonists of the twentieth century, and also by those who simply want to enjoy the very best in visual humour.

Other Titles in the Prion Cartoon Classics Series

Nicolas Bentley

David Langdon (forthcoming)

Leslie Starke (forthcoming)

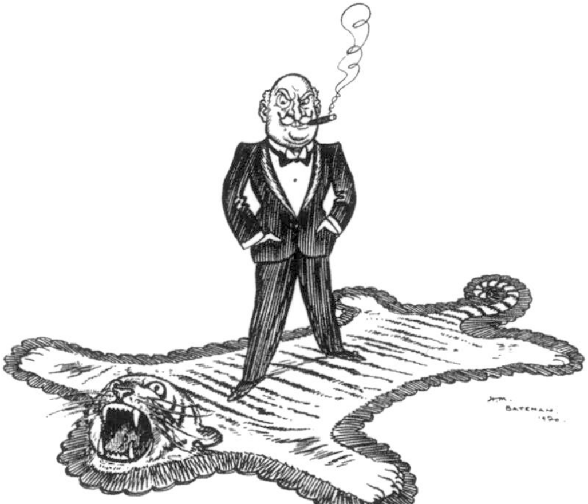
H.M. BATEMAN

H.M. Bateman

Edited by Mark Bryant

PRION

First published in 2002
Reprinted 2003 by

Prion Books
an imprint of the
Carlton Publishing Group
20 Mortimer Street
London W1T 3JW

A catalogue record for this book is available from the British Library

ISBN 1-85375-458-7

Printed and bound in China
by Everbest Printing Co. Ltd

Foreword

by George Melly

H. M. Bateman was born in Australia where his father had lived for some years in the saddle and wielded the stockwhip, but before he was two his formidable mother commanded a return to England where the family settled for suburban gentility 'outside the four-mile radius'.

He became, in consequence, the reluctant poet of expanding Metroland, the Cassandra of Clapham. He harboured, however, a wistful admiration for 'Bohemia' – that is to say, not washing up after meals during his training or later on by joining the Savage Club or the Chelsea Arts. Politically he was predictably reactionary but harboured real sympathy for the underdog. The victim of many of his cartoons is, in fact, himself, recognizable by his large blobby nose acquired by his insistence on boxing as a boy, despite having no talent for it whatsoever.

I think that some of his earlier full-page drawings for the *Sketch* are (as drawings) amongst his finest but commercial demands may have cut back the time available for such thoughtful one-offs. Never less than confident and often inspired, his later drawings became coarser – more predictable. By 1914 he seemed to be published everywhere, but the war threw him. Soon invalided out of the army he felt what he called 'a hopeless dud', but was in part comforted when he discovered that a rather savage drawing he did of bayonet practice was used as a means of encouragement during training.

The war over, he entered his years of triumph. He had 'created the taste to appreciate him' and his invention was running at full throttle. He had also begun to establish certain characters, a choleric colonel in particular, who became tremendously popular. There is indeed one drawing centring on a colonel losing his temper at golf which suggests that at times Bateman may have gone wonderfully mad. The retired military man is swearing. All those around him have swooned or are perhaps dead, but that is not all. Out of the Colonel's mouth emerges a kind of obscene pink bubble, a 'thing' with several eyes and protuberances, giving out puffs of smoke and with a single bump covered in sparse hairs. This Dali-like creature, this horrific manifest curse, has split the heavens into Futurist shards. (Bateman, incidentally, detested modern art after Impressionism, although in old age he was very moved to meet Cezanne's son.)

Yet Bateman's comparative immortality, far surpassing his contemporaries, rests on 'The Man Who...' phenomenon. The idea is very simple. You take a situation where conventional behaviour is *de rigueur*, and then expose an individual who unknowingly ignores it. Thus: 'The Man who Crept into the Royal Enclosure in a Bowler', 'The Man Who Lit his Cigar Before the Loyal Toast' etc. These, and many cartoons using the same format if not the actual verbal phrases, became a national obsession, but why? Was it perhaps Bateman's own social insecurity which confronted those who had recently become middle class? It was no doubt, of course, in some cases a useful hint. Yet there is a savagery and cruelty in it. The eyeballs of those who know the conventions start from their heads, their owners swell in size and turn purple with rage. Meanwhile their victim, if already aware of his transgression, shrinks into insignificance.

By all accounts H. M. Bateman was an eccentric in his private life. He had a terror and hatred of the Inland Revenue that verged on paranoia and there were difficulties with his family that led to his spending his final years on the island of Gozo, Malta. However, it cannot be denied that he had a remarkable talent. A genius, according to Bertrand Russell, is someone who, however slightly, alters our view of the world. H. M. Bateman, that strange, shy, complicated. unaffectionate eye, was one who did.

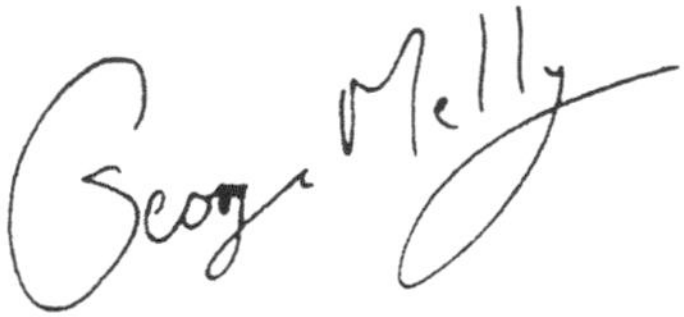

Contents

Editor's Note

It is always difficult to know what to include and what to leave out in a compilation of this sort and ultimately the choice has been a personal one. Also, for maximum quality of reproduction and to keep within a workable publishing budget black-and-white line drawings have mostly been used, though I am very pleased that we have been able to include a small colour section as well. The drawings have largely been taken from the main cartoon anthologies published in Bateman's lifetime – *Burlesques* (1916), *A Book of Drawings* (1921), *Suburbia* (1922), *More Drawings* (1922), *A Mixture* (1924), *Colonels* (1925), *Rebound* (1927), *Brought Forward* (1931) and *Considered Trifles* (1934). By concentrating on the books this also has the advantage that these drawings would have been among those of which Bateman himself would have approved.

For help in the preparation of this book I am greatly indebted to Bateman's daughter Diana Willis and her husband Dick, both for their practical assistance with regard to checking facts and the loan of material but also more their constant encouragement and support. Thanks also go to Anthony Anderson, John Jensen, Michael Bateman and Mark Boxer whose own books, *The Man Who Was H.M. Bateman* (1982), *The Man Who...and Other Drawings* (1975), *The Man Who Drew the Twentieth Century* (1969) and *The Best of H.M.Bateman*: *The Tatler Cartoons* 1922-26, respectively — now all sadly out of print – have been a source of much inspiration. In addition, my thanks go to George Melly for agreeing to write the Foreword. And last but not least, many thanks to Barry Winkleman and Jim Pope of Prion Books for producing such a handsome book.

M.B.

Introduction

H. M. Bateman (1887-1970) was most celebrated for his 'The Man Who...' series of cartoons featuring hilarious social gaffes in which some lonely, embarrassed figure commits a ghastly *faux pas* to the amazement or outrage of the assembled onlookers. Such classic drawings as 'The Man Who Lit His Cigar Before the Loyal Toast', 'The Guardsman Who Dropped It' and 'The Boy Who Breathed on the Glass at the British Museum' – all published long before the Second World War – are as fresh today as when they first appeared and have earned Bateman a permanent place in the cartoonists' hall of fame and international celebrity that will last for generations to come.

Henry Mayo Bateman was born at 'Moss Vale' in the village of Sutton Forest, near Goulburn, New South Wales, Australia on 15 February 1887. He was the son of Henry Charles Bateman, an English-born cattle rancher, and Rose Mayo, the daughter of a Brixton building contractor whom his father had met and married on a trip to England in 1885. In 1889, when Henry was only 18 months old, the family returned, at his mother's insistence, to England where his younger sister Phyllis was born the following year. Here his father bought an export packing and shipping business in Golden Heart Wharf, Upper Thames Street, near Blackfriars Bridge, London, and settled his family at first in Romford, Essex, and then Honor Oak, south London.

Bateman attended Forest Hill House School, Forest Hill, where his first published drawings – a series of postcards – were produced, signed 'Binks' (his family pet-name). His father hoped he'd follow him into the family firm but in 1901 his mother sent some of his drawings to the famous cartoonist and illustrator Phil May who was impressed and suggested he study drawing and painting in a year or so's time at Westminster School of Art under May's friend Mouat Loudan. Meanwhile, he continued to produce cartoons, largely influenced by the artists of the weekly *Comic Cuts*, *Ally Sloper's Half Holiday*, *Punch* and *Fun* (which his

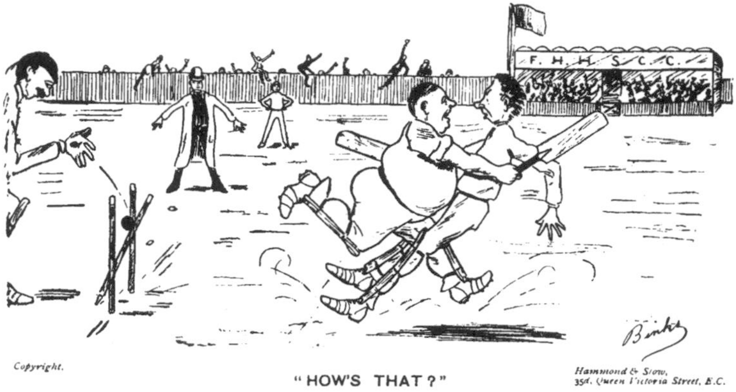
F. H. H. S. C. C.
Binks
Copyright.
"HOW'S THAT?"
Hammond & Stow,
35d, Queen Victoria Street, E.C.

One of Bateman's first published cartoons, signed 'Binks' and reproduced as a postcard while he was still at school.

father took). His first drawings began to appear in comic papers in 1902 at the age of 15 and by the following year he was regularly being published (as 'H.M.Bateman') in *Scraps*, *Comic Life* and *Chips*.

Bateman left school aged 16 and went, as planned, to Westminster School of Art for nine months (1903) and then studied at the Goldsmiths' Institute, New Cross (1903-5), under Frederick Marriot. It was Marriot who helped Bateman get his first commission, an advertisement for a paper company for which he was paid 1½ guineas. A fellow student at Goldsmith's was Sir Ernest Shackleton's older sister, who introduced Bateman to a contact of hers at the publishers C. A. Pearson. As a result Bateman finally broke away from comics and got a commission for ten cartoons and two story illustrations in Pearson's monthly *Royal Magazine* (1904). Work for *London Opinion* and the prestigious weekly the *Tatler* followed the same year.

At about this time Bateman got to know (through some friends at the

Westminster School of Art) the celebrated poster artist John Hassall. In 1905, when Hassall's former tutor Charles van Havermaet left Holland and set up a studio in Earl's Court, Bateman, on Hassall's recommendation, decided to leave Goldsmith's and join him. He remained at the studio for nearly three years while still living at home with his parents (by then in Clapham). By the time he was 18 he was contributing regularly to the *Bystander* (1905), the *Sketch* (full-page cartoons from 1905), *Printer's Pie* (1905), *Windsor Magazine* (1906), *Pearson's Weekly* (1907) and others.

In 1907, struggling with the decision whether to become a serious painter or a cartoonist and illustrator, Bateman suffered a nervous collapse. However, he soon recovered and, the decision made, left Van Havermaet's studio, turned his back on academic art and took on A.E.Johnson (who also represented Heath Robinson, Fougasse and others) as his agent. By 1909 he was publishing three new cartoons every week, a rate he kept up until the outbreak of the First World War. During this period he also contributed to *Lady's Realm* (1908), *Granta* (1910) and other publications, succeeded Norman Morrow (elder brother of George Morrow, later to become Art Editor of *Punch*) as theatre caricaturist for the *Bystander* (1910-12) and from 1912 to 1914 produced regular full-page theatre caricatures for the *Sketch* (as 'Our Untamed Artist at the Play'). He also designed theatre posters, notably for the successful 1912 West End productions of George Bernard Shaw's *Fanny's First Play* and *John Bull's Other Island*. His first exhibition was held in 1911 at the Brook Street Gallery, London.

In the First World War Bateman volunteered to join the army, serving briefly in the London Regiment before being invalided out with rheumatic fever in 1915. Returning to live with his parents (now settled in Bromley, Kent), he then began drawing for *Punch*. His first cartoon for the magazine, 'The Boy Who Breathed on the Glass at the British Museum' (4 October 1916, and now owned by the museum), brought him lasting fame and Arnold Bennett would later describe him as 'the one really humorous first-class draughtsman in *Punch*'. His first book, *Burlesques* (1916), also appeared the same year and at about this time he also produced some 800 drawings for a pioneering animated cartoon, long before Disney. During the war Bateman drew some of his most famous black-and-white cartoons such as 'It's the Same Man', 'The Recruit Who Took to it Kindly', 'The Spot', 'Love at First Sight' and 'Prisoner When Arrested Clung to the Railings', the last of which *Punch* printed over two whole pages in an ordinary single issue (they later went further and published 'The One Note Man' – probably Bateman's most elaborate drawing and involving 58 incidents – as four pages). During this period he also met and became lifelong friends with the writer William Caine (who features in many of his drawings) and the painter and war artist Philip Connard RA.

By 1919 Bateman's fame was such that queues formed for an exhibition of his work at the Leicester Galleries, London (*The Times* said his drawings had 'a comic beauty of line, a rhythmical extravagance like that of the *Ingoldsby Legends* and the choruses of Offenbach'), and ten collections of his cartoons were published between 1916 and 1934. In 1922 he drew for the *Tatler* what was probably his most popular single cartoon 'The Guardsman Who Dropped It', a colour centre-spread drawing for which he was paid 200 guineas (a sum then unheard of for a cartoon and equivalent to the annual stipend of a curate). The success of this led to the famous 'The Man Who...' series of colour cartoons for the magazine, which were also produced as prints. (Though the series is perhaps best known from the *Tatler*, Bateman himself dates it from 'The Missed Putt' published in 1912.) In addition, black-and-white variants on the same theme appeared in *Punch* together with a number of popular cartoon advertising campaigns using the concept, notably those for Colman's Mustard, Kensitas Cigarettes, Lucky Strike, Wills Tobacco, Moss Bros, Guinness, New World Cookers, Erasmic Soap, Simpson's Restaurant, Shell and Lloyd's amongst others. After the war he also had considerable success with jokes featuring apoplectic colonels (pre-dating Low's 'Colonel Blimp' character by a decade or so) and a book of these, *Colonels*, was published in 1925.

After his parents split up in 1922 Bateman built a house in Reigate, Surrey, and lived there with his mother and sister. A member of the Chelsea Arts Club

H. M. Bateman in
the 1920s.

since 1910 (proposed by the cartoonist Frank Hart) he met his future wife, Brenda Mary Collison Weir at the Chelsea Arts Ball in 1925. They were married on 29 September 1926 (he was 39, she was 16 years younger). Her mother was the cousin of another Chelsea Arts Club member, Harry Collison (who shared a house with Bateman's friend the cartoonist Fred Pegram), and it was Collison who introduced them. After their marriage the couple moved into the house in Reigate (Bateman's mother and sister moved out) and they had two daughters, Diana (born 1927) and Monica (born 1929).

Bateman exhibited at the Royal Academy in 1933 and paintings from a Spanish trip were shown at the Leicester Galleries in 1936. The same year he also published a book, *The Art of Caricature*. Then, while still only in his forties, Bateman decided to retire and concentrated on becoming a 'serious' artist – his last cartoon for *Punch* appeared in 1934 (though after a 14-year gap some 1930s drawings were published in the magazine in 1948) and his last one for the *Tatler* in 1936. His final cartoon collection, *Considered Trifles*, also appeared in 1934. For the next thirty years or so his income derived largely from royalties on his published work plus occasional writings and sales of paintings. In 1937 he wrote an autobiography, *H. M. Bateman by Himself* (which was serialized in the *News Chronicle*), and soon after published a travel book, *On the Move in England* (1940, serialized in the *Sunday Times*).

During the Second World War Bateman served as an air-raid warden and drew a few cartoons for Government ministries (notably the 'Cough and Sneezes Spread Diseases' series for the Ministry of Health) but otherwise continued to focus on painting in oils and watercolour (in 1943 he even enrolled in classes at the Ruskin College of Fine Art in Oxford to improve his technique). However, by 1946 he had become increasingly unwell and somewhat paranoid (particularly about the Inland Revenue) and as a result the family split up in 1947. He then lived alone in various parts of Britain before settling in 1953 in Sampford Courtenay, Devon, on the edge of Dartmoor. Here he became a virtual recluse, painting and writing, notably *The Evening Rise* (1956), a book on fly-fishing.

Bateman detested modern art (especially Matisse, Picasso and the Cubists) but was a great admirer of the work of the caricaturists Henry Ospovat and Max Beerbohm, the Russian-born French cartoonist Emmanuel Poiré ('Caran D'Ache') and the artists of the German satirical magazine *Simplicissimus*. He once said that he tried to draw people not as they *looked* but as they *felt* and rarely used captions or speech-bubbles. An accomplished draughtsman, his sense of humour often verged on the surreal, a combination described by G. K. Chesterton in his Foreword to Bateman's *A Book of Drawings* (1921) as 'wild exactitude'. The cartoonist Mark Boxer has also compared his story-without-words strips to mime and called them 'the pen and ink equivalent of the routines of Chaplin or Jacques Tati'.

As well as publishing his own collections, Bateman illustrated more than 20 books including titles by Lewis Carroll, William Caine and George Robey and drew for a wide variety of publications including the *Passing Show, London Calling, Piccadilly, Radio Times* (including covers), *Strand, Eve, Nash's Magazine, Humorist, Land & Water, Sunday Graphic, Illustrated Sporting & Dramatic News*, the *Field* (sports cartoons, 1935–7) and others, as well as such foreign journals as *Rions* and *La Baïonnette* (France), *Calendar* (Germany) and *Life*, *New Yorker* and the *Sportsman* (USA). In addition he was a member of the London Sketch Club and the Savage and in 1949 read a paper to the Royal Society of Arts entitled 'Humour in Art' in which he proposed the establishment of a National Gallery of Humorous Art. (Sadly this was not achieved in his lifetime, though since his death his eldest daughter Diana has done much to promote this idea through the activities of the Cartoon Art Trust, of which she is a founder director.)

In 1962 an exhibition at the Fine Art Society, London, suddenly brought Bateman's cartoon work back into vogue and in 1964 he came out of retirement to receive the accolades of a new generation of admirers, including an award from the Cartoonists' Club of Great Britain. However, despite this renewed celebrity he became increasingly unhappy in Britain and continued to travel in search of a spot that would be better for his health and help his painting. Eventually he moved to Malta and settled on the nearby island of Gozo. Here he spent his remaining years in the Royal Lady Hotel, Mgarr. H.M.Bateman died while out walking on Gozo on 11 February 1970 and was buried in the British cemetery, Malta.

Since his death Bateman's reputation has continued to grow. A centenary exhibition of his work was held at the Royal Festival Hall and the National Theatre in 1987 and examples of his drawings are currently held in the collections of the Victoria & Albert Museum, the British Museum Prints & Drawings Department, the National Portrait Gallery, the Ashmolean Museum, the University of Kent Cartoon Centre and elsewhere. And in 1997 an English Heritage commemorative Blue Plaque was erected to his memory on his house in Clapham, London.

Mark Bryant
London, 2002

The Armed Forces

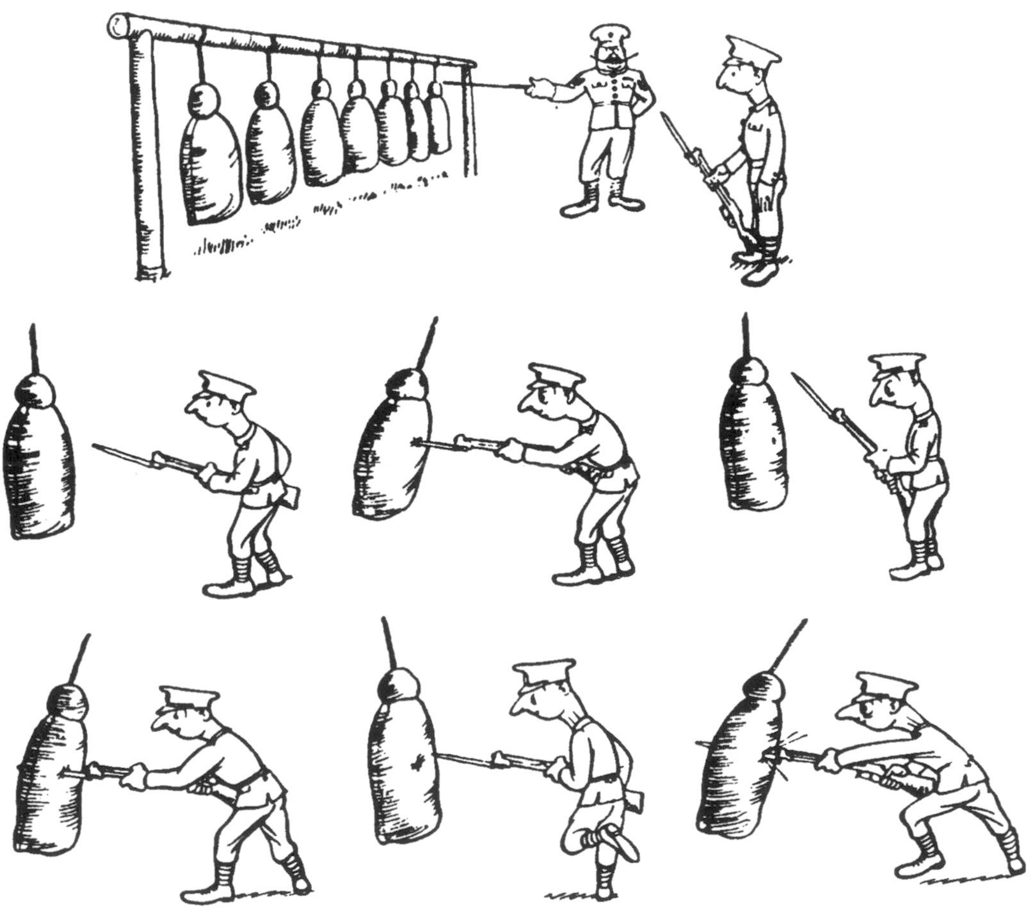

The Recruit Who Took to it Kindly

H.M. BATEMAN 16

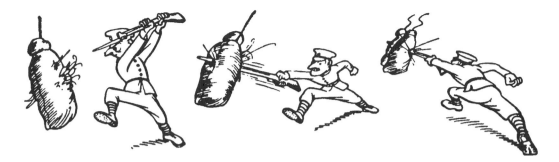

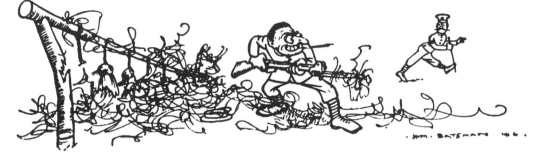

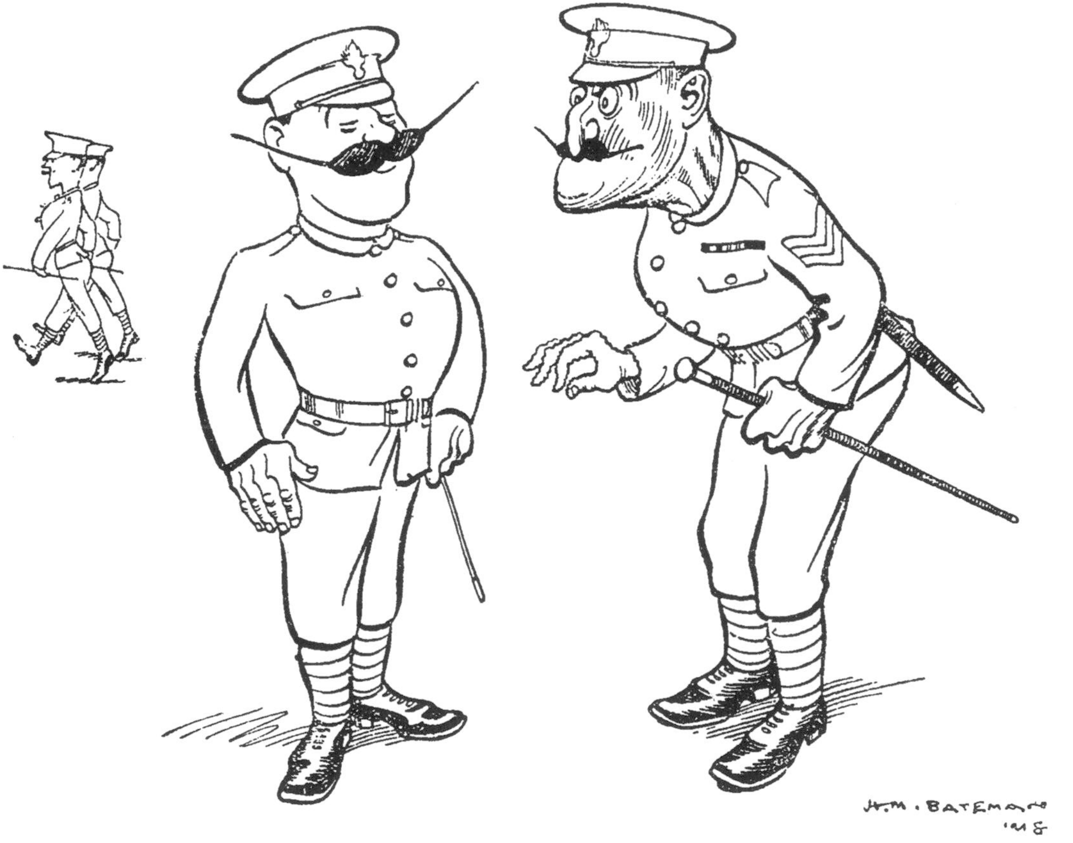
H.M. BATEMAN
1918

Deeds That Ought to Win the VC

The Private Grows a Better One Than the Sergeant

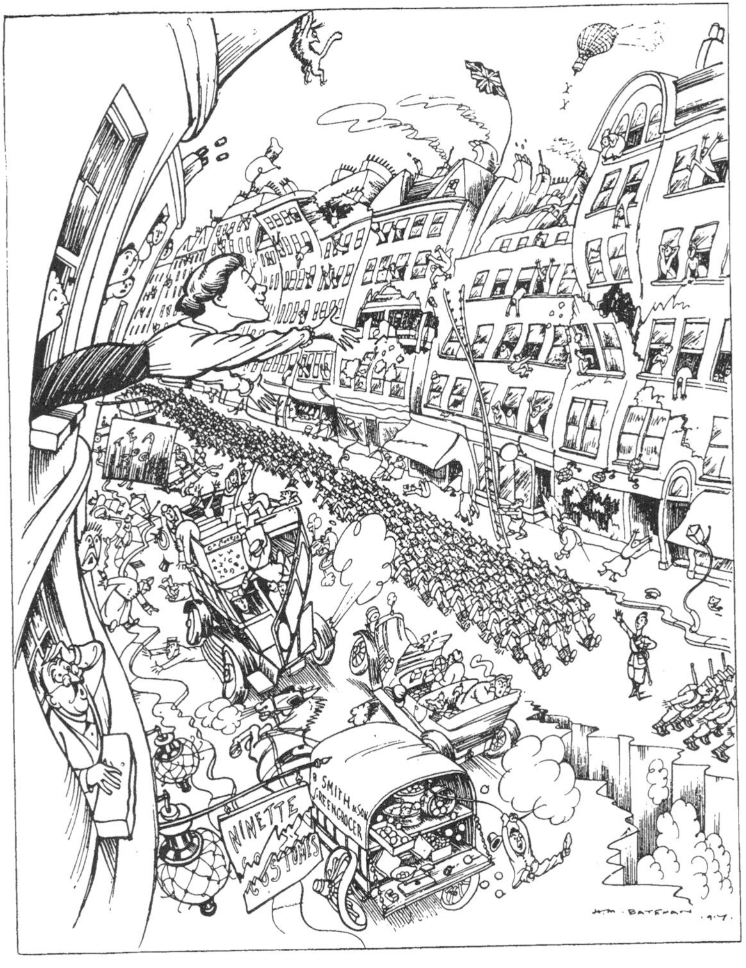
B SMITH & SON
GREENGROCER
NINETTE
COSTUMES
H.M. BATEMAN .917.

Love at First Sight – Its Disturbing Influence

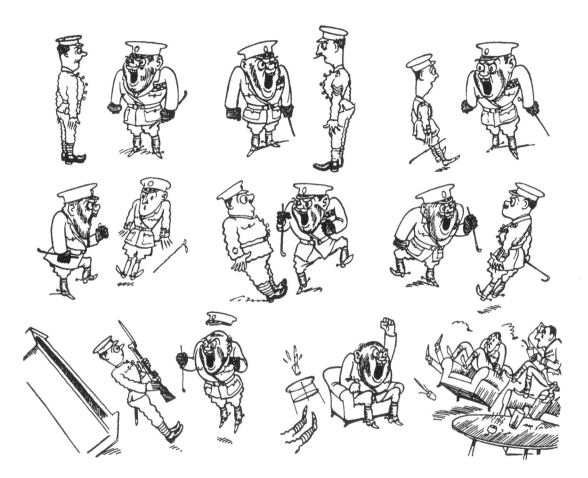

The CO – A Man's Man

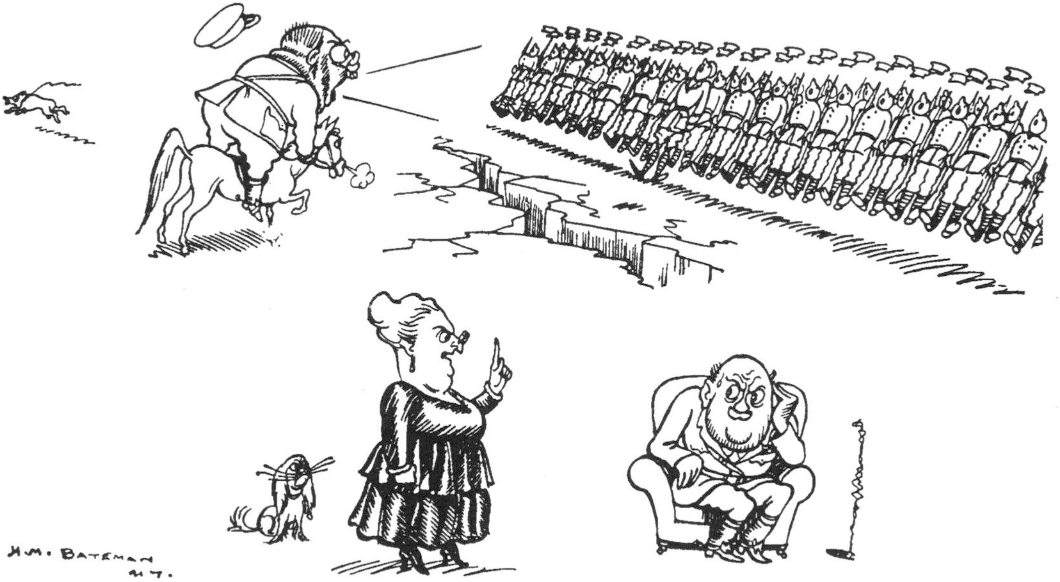
H.M. BATEMAN
47.

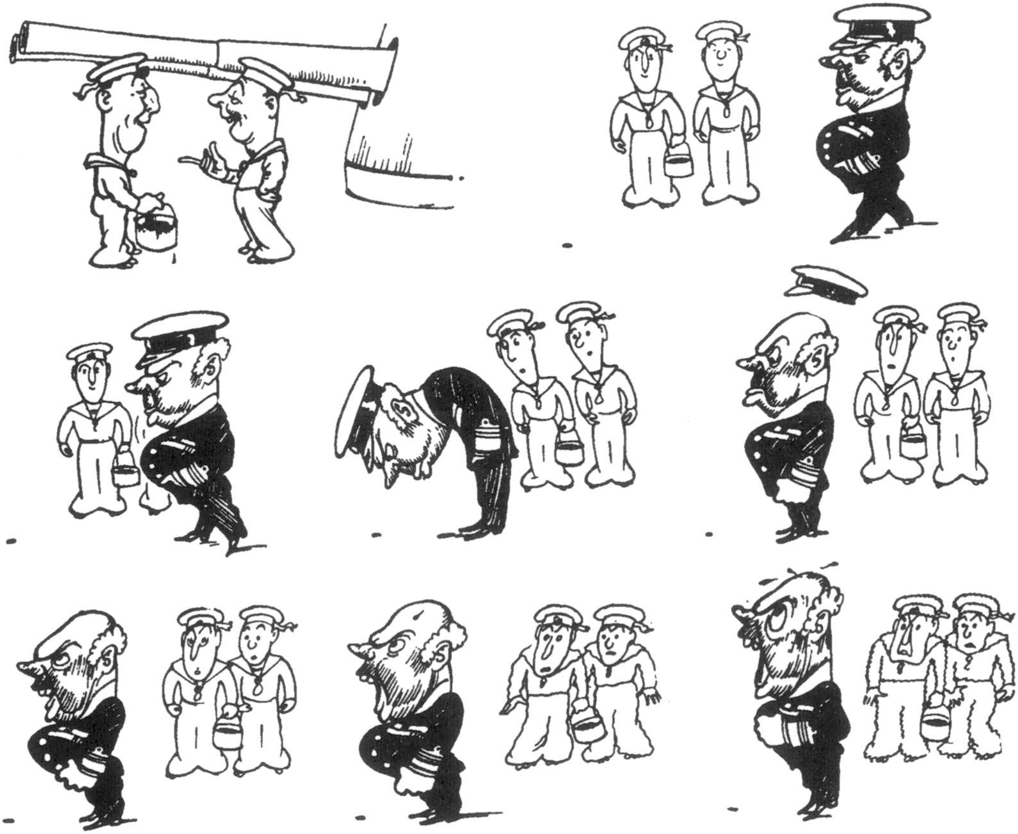

The 'Damned Spot'

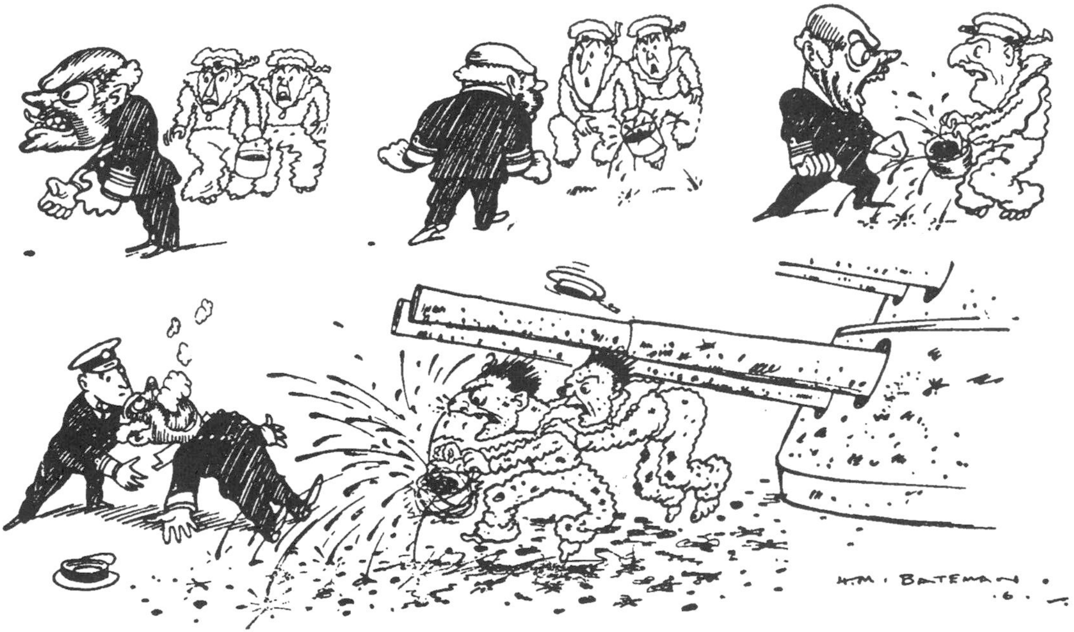
H.M. BATEMAN

The Politician Who Addressed the Troops

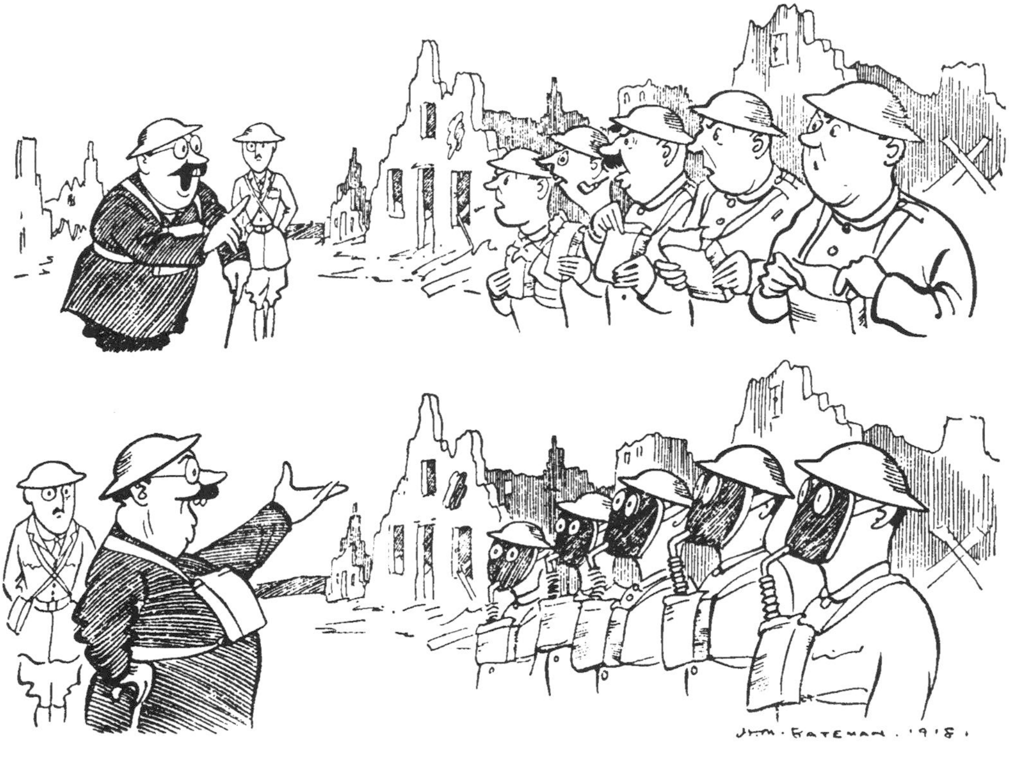
H.M. BATEMAN. 1918.

It's the Same Man!

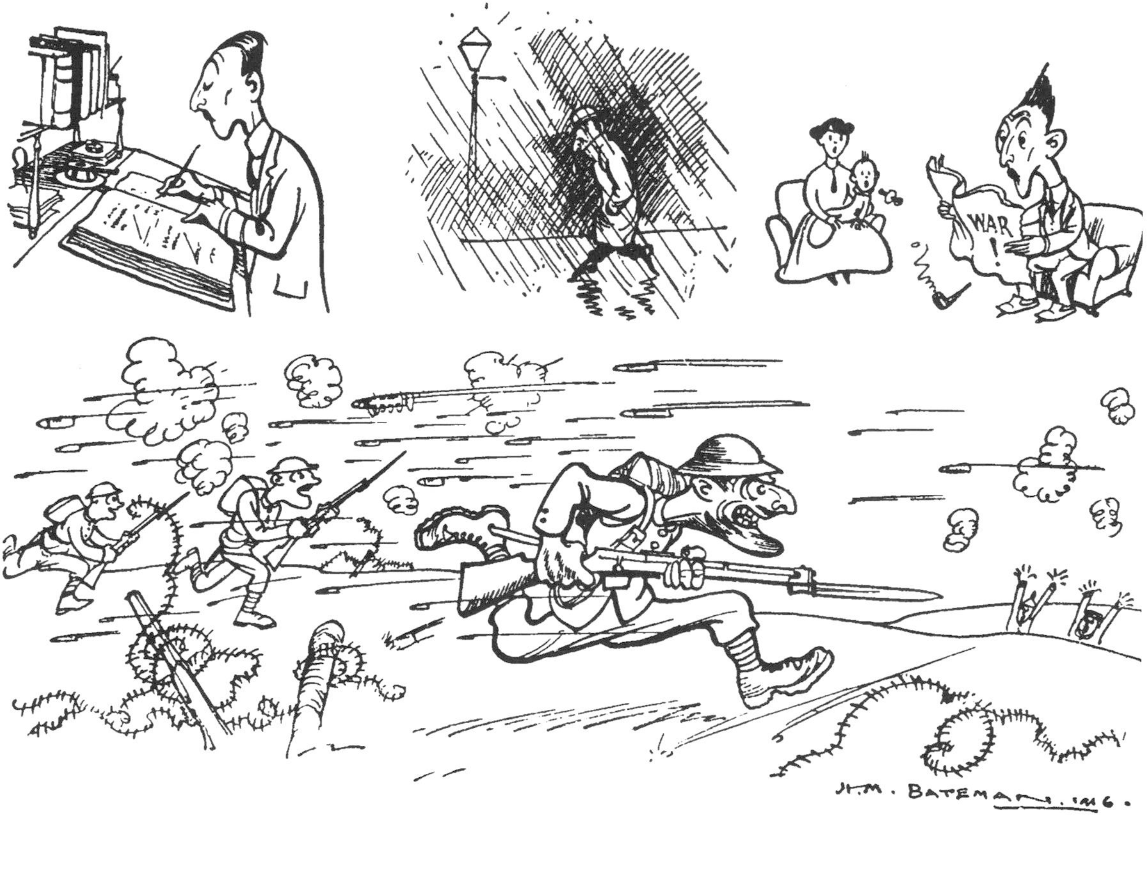
WAR !
H.M. BATEMAN. 1916.

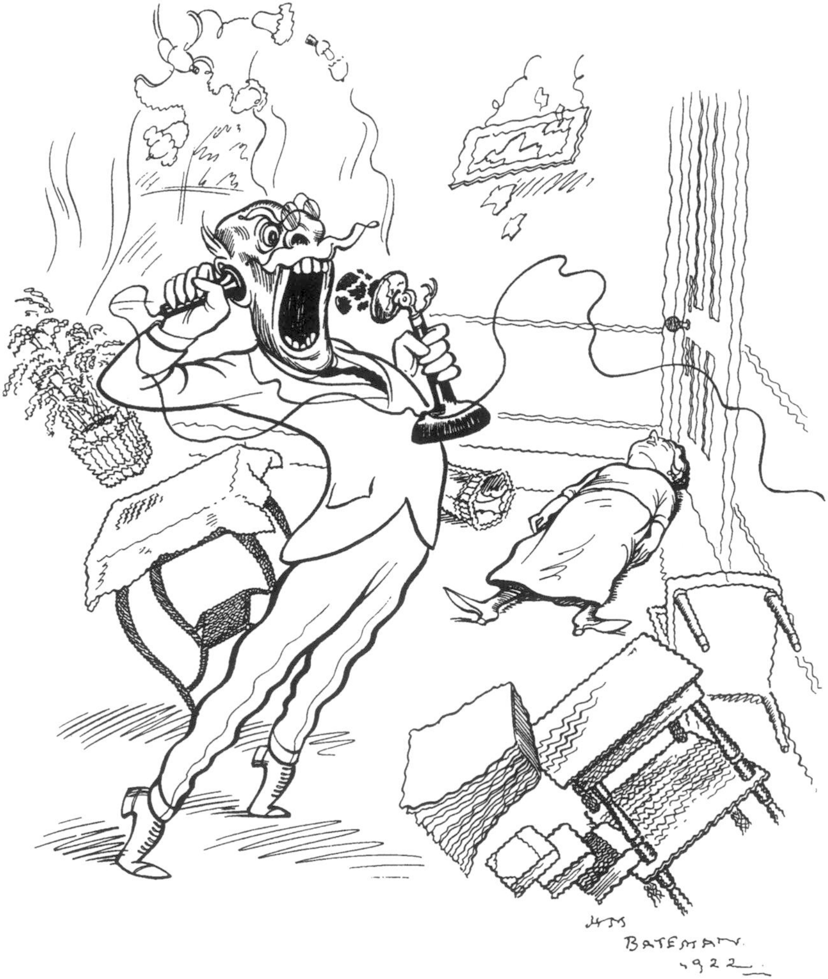
H M
BATEMAN
1922

The Colonel Talks to the Exchange

Something in the City

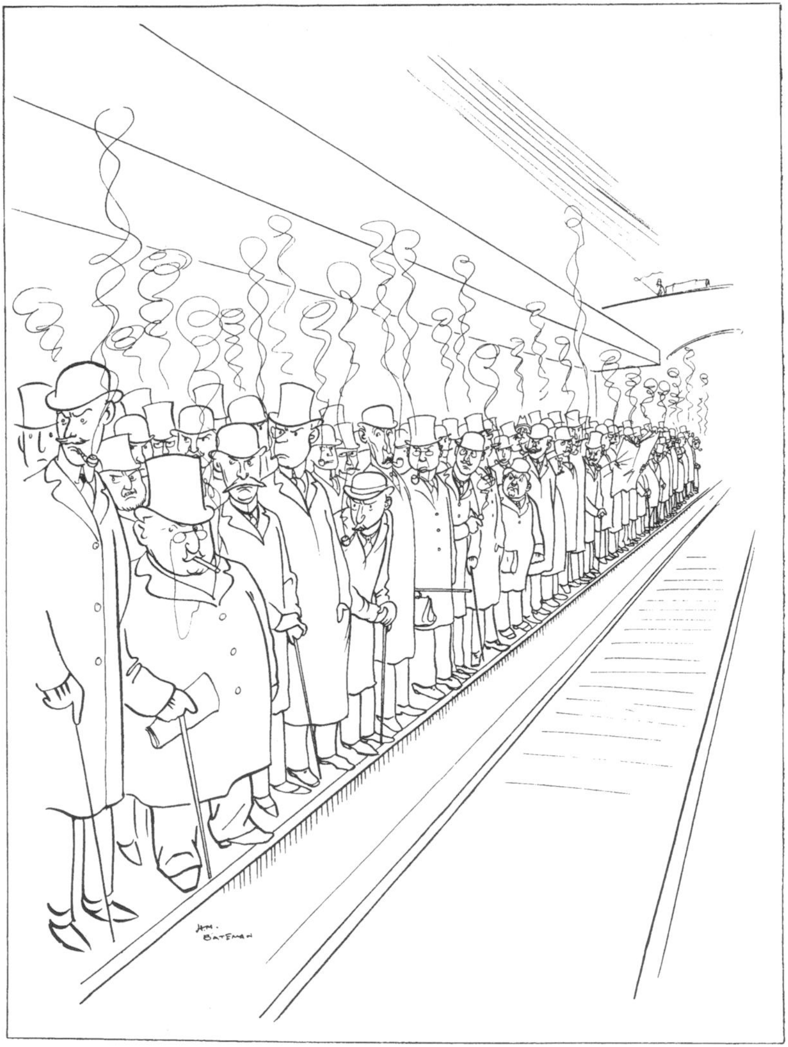
H.M.
BATEMAN

The 8.45

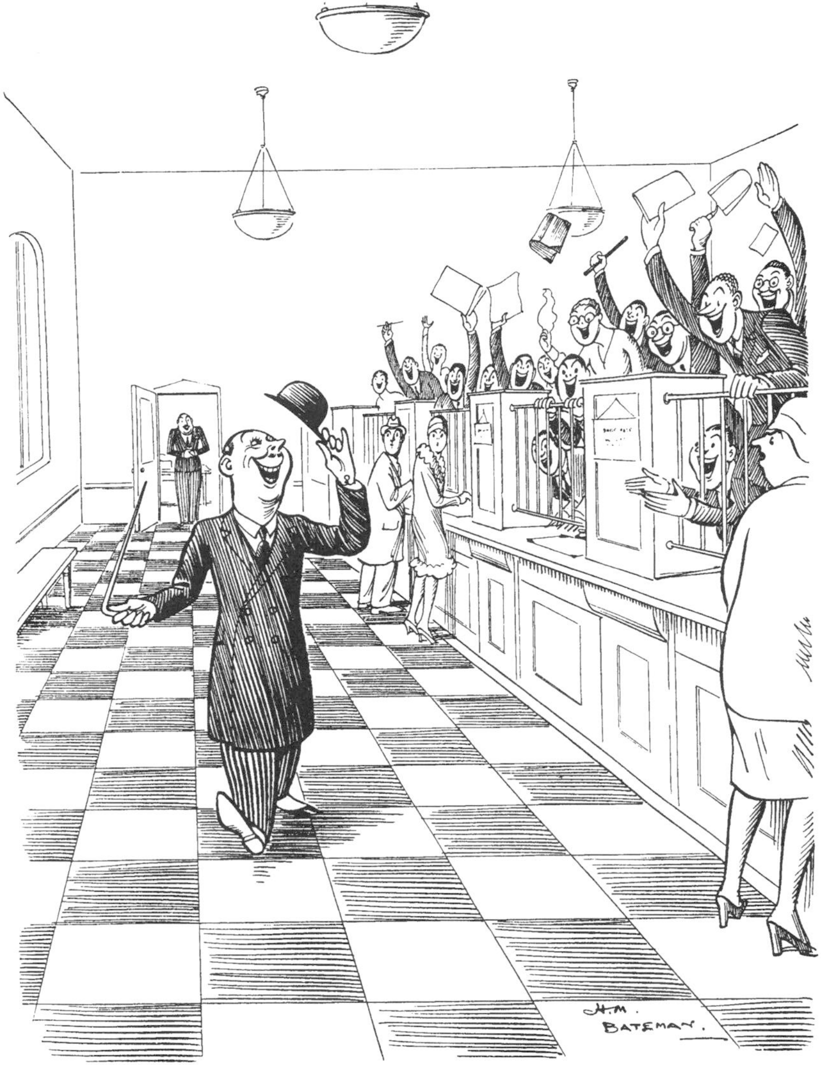
H.M. BATEMAN.

The Man Who Paid Off His Overdraft

Iron Trousers

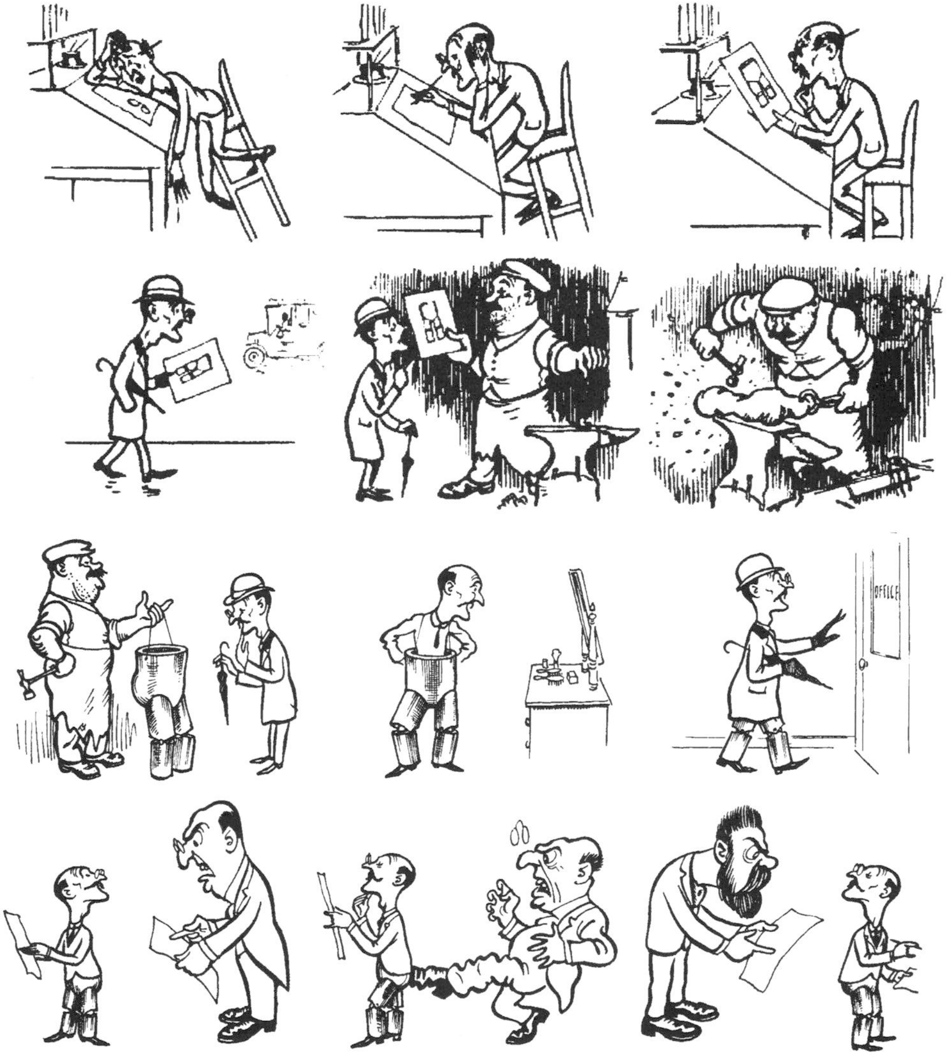
OFFICE

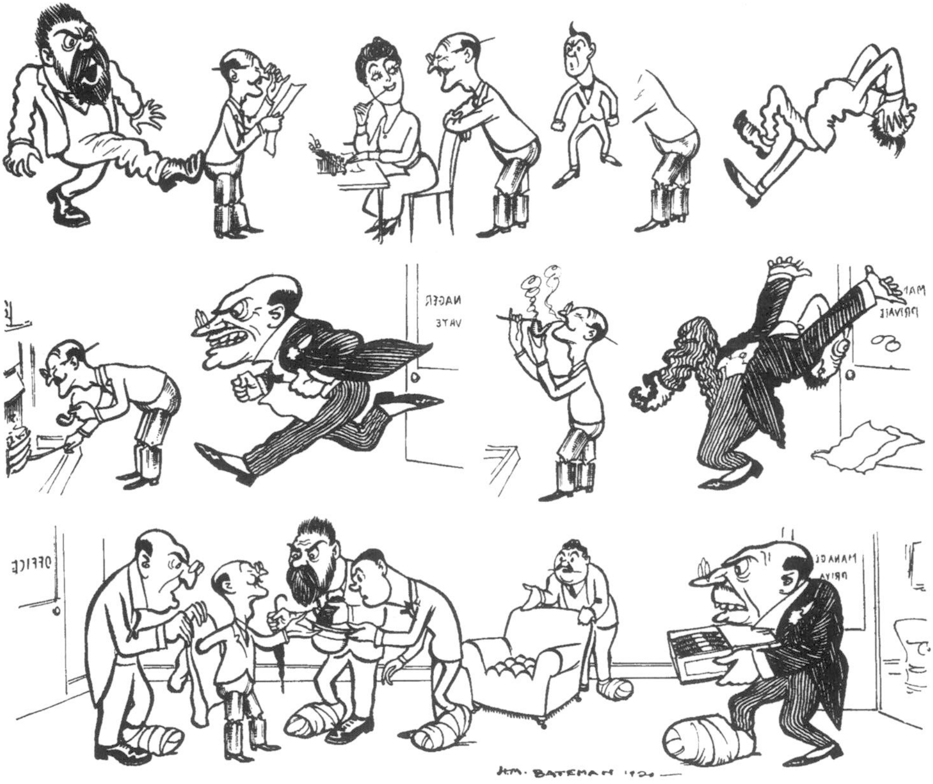
H.M. BATEMAN 1920

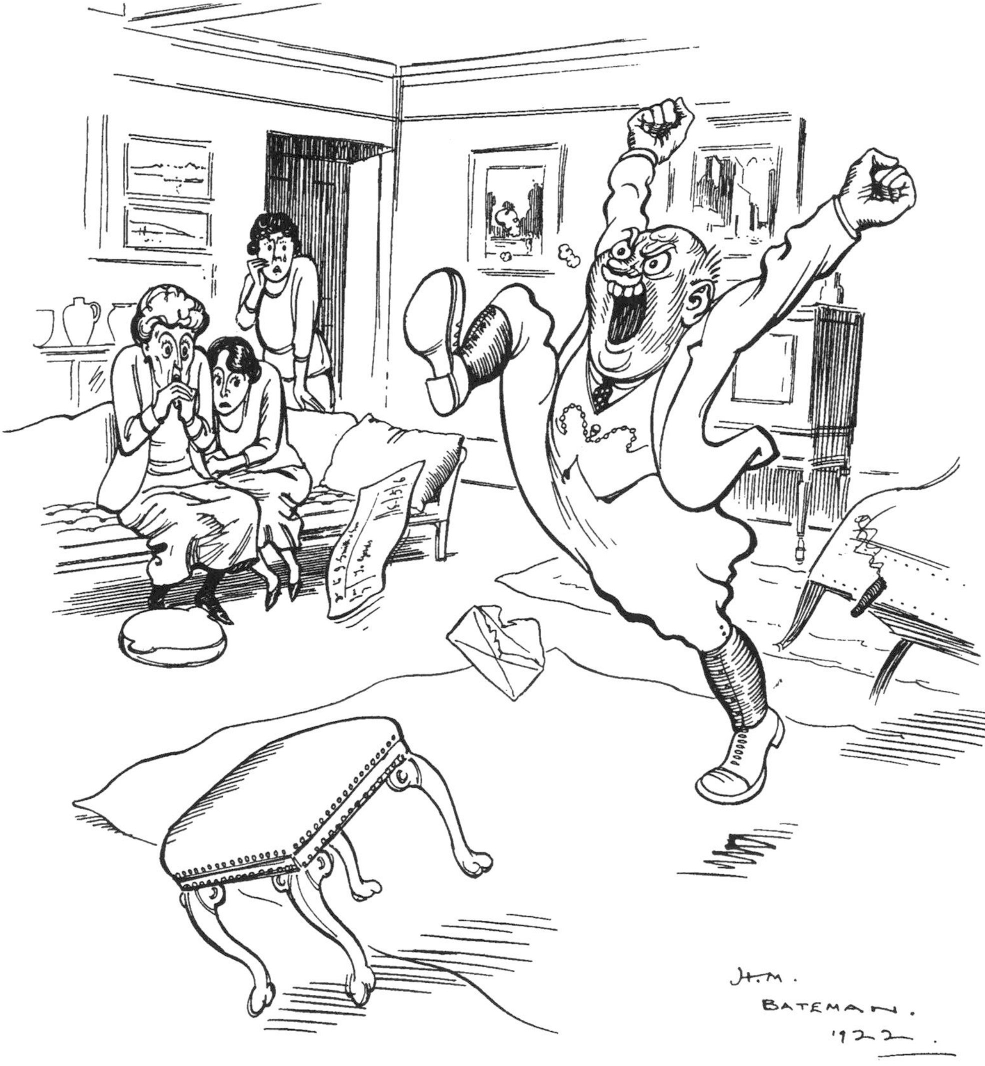
H.M.
BATEMAN.
1922.

'To Account Rendered'

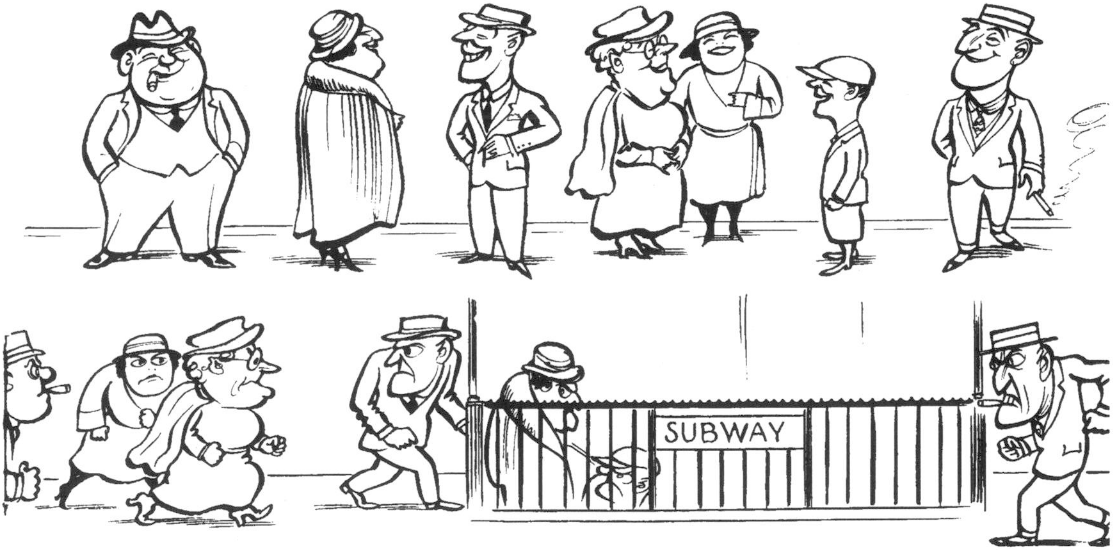
SUBWAY

Environment

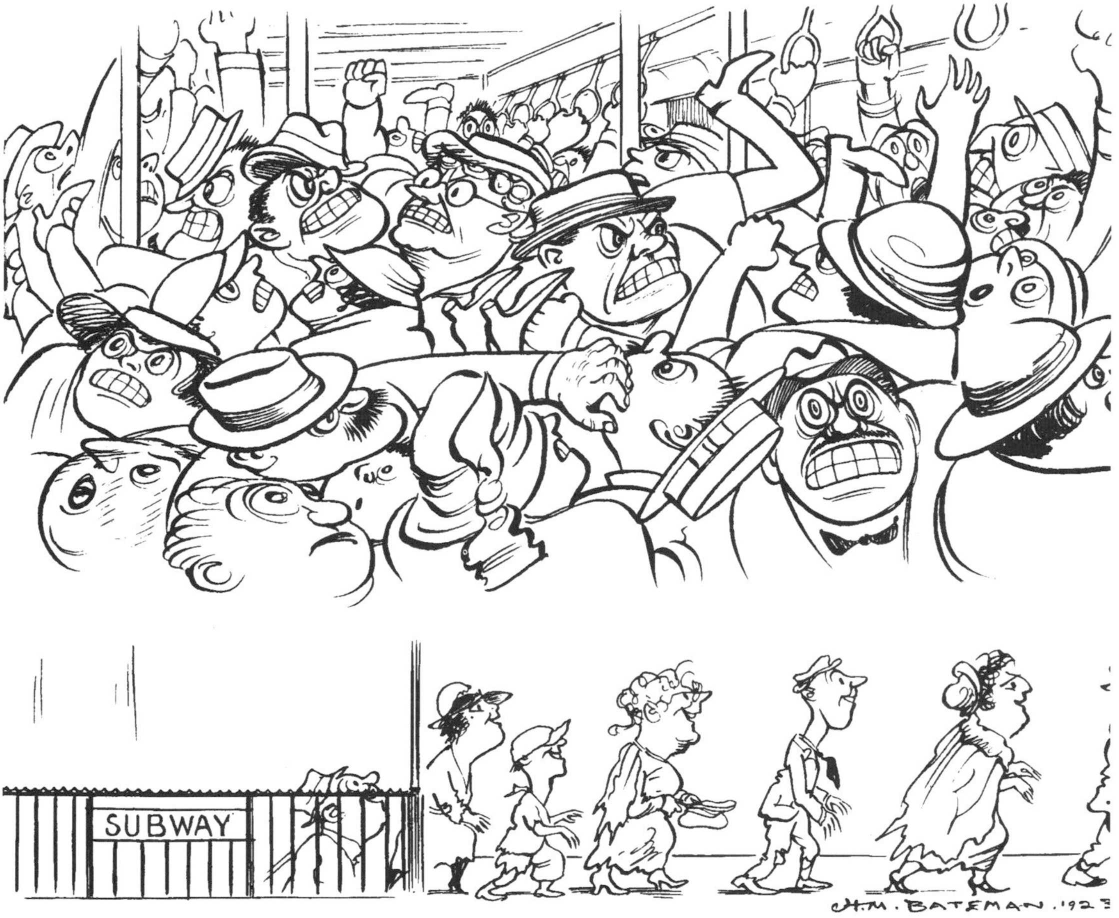
SUBWAY
H.M. BATEMAN

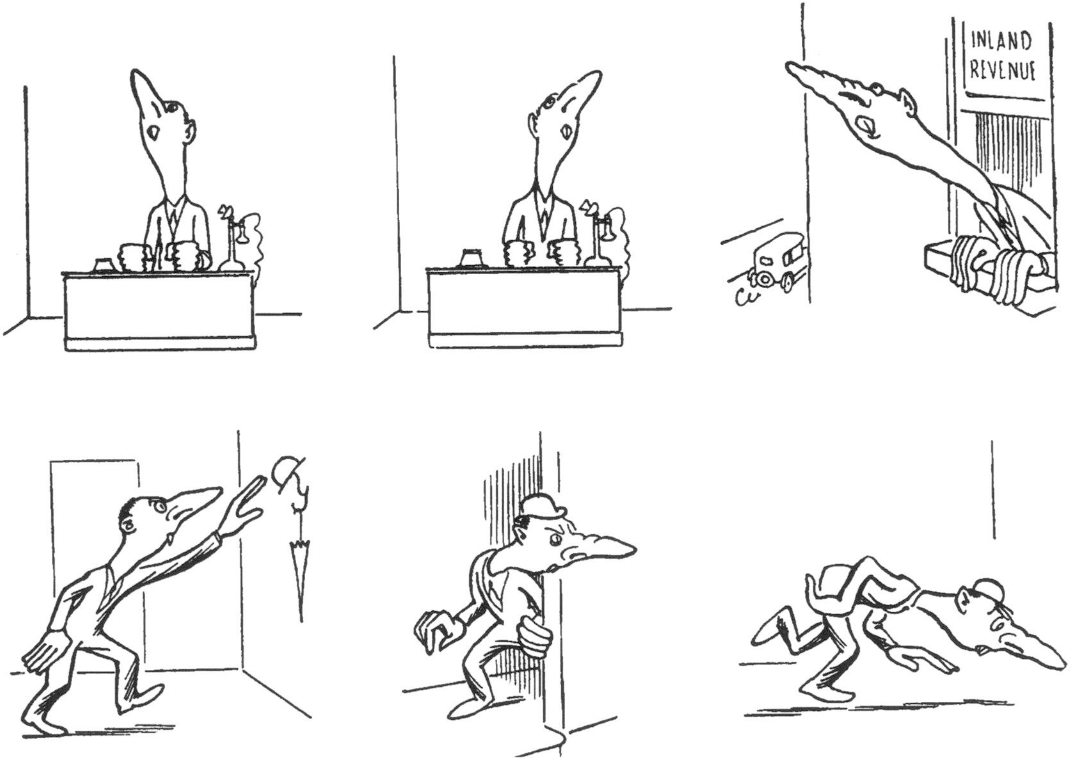
INLAND
REVENUE

An Income Tax Official Tracking a Halfpenny

BATEMAN

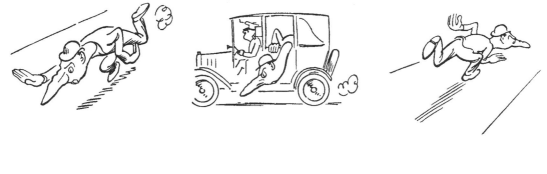

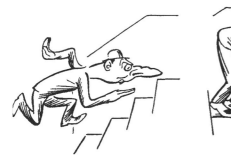

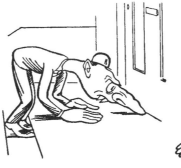

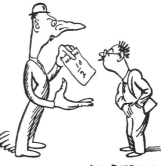

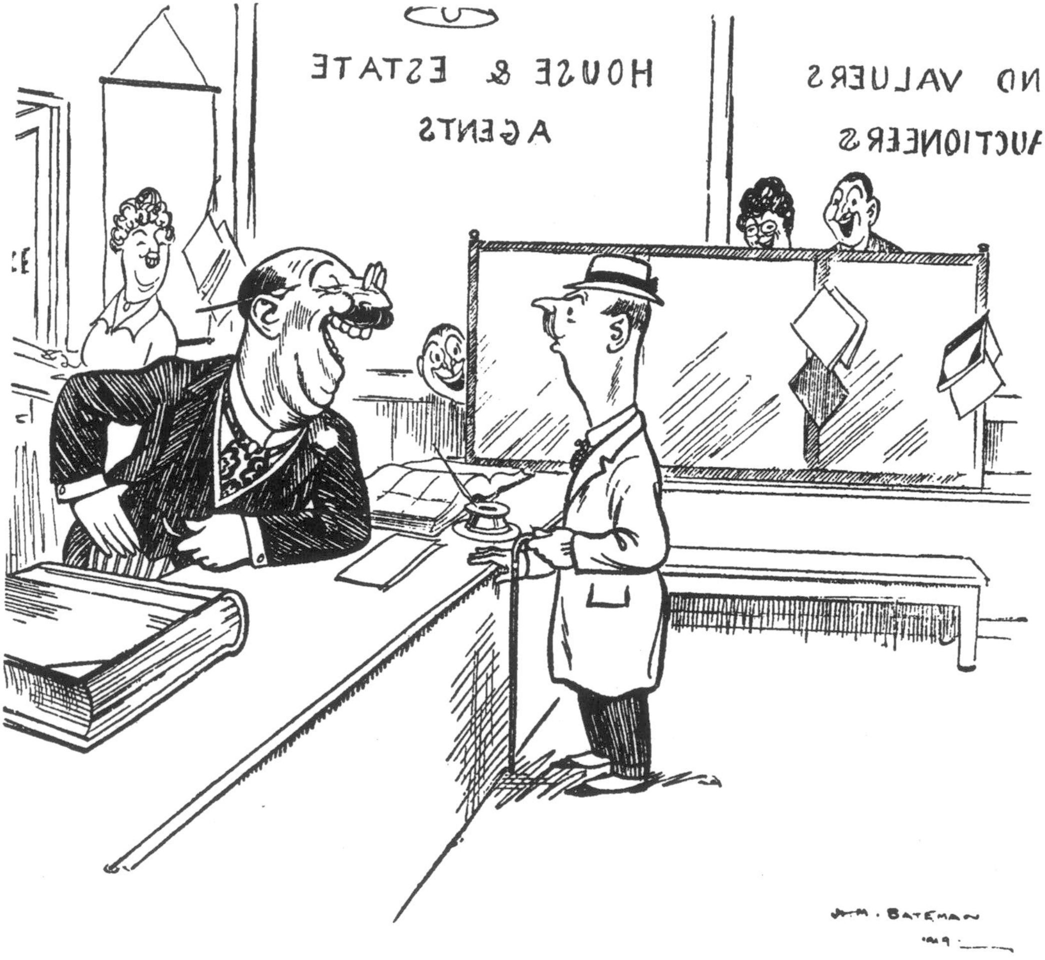
HOUSE & ESTATE
AGENTS
ND VALUERS
UCTIONEERS
H.M. BATEMAN

The Man Who Asked a House-Agent if He Had any Houses to Let

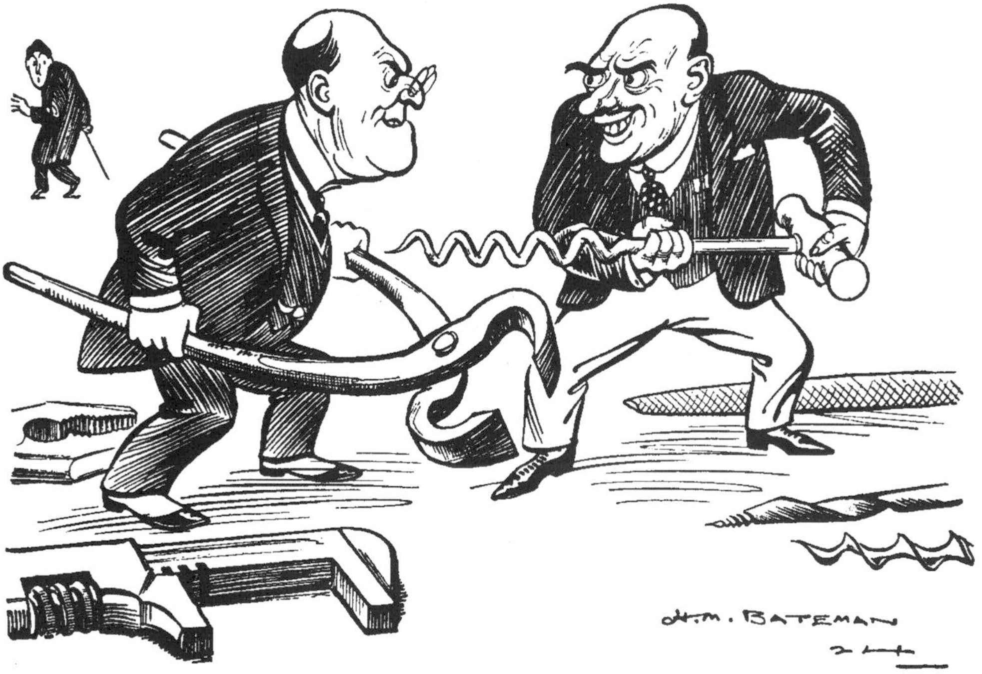
H.M. BATEMAN

Two Commissioners of Inland Revenue Comparing Methods

The Assessment

The Sporting Life

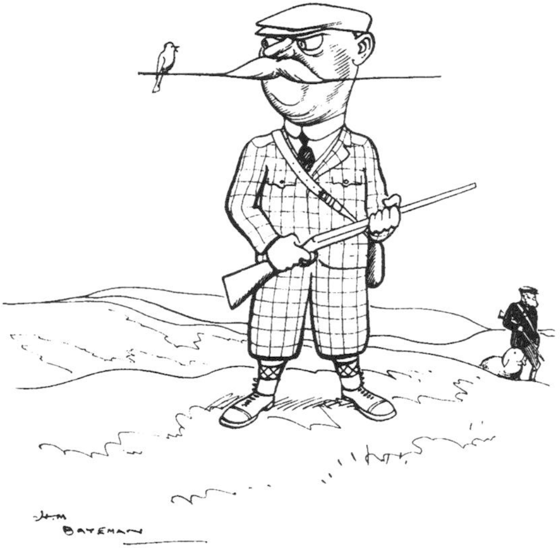
H.M BATEMAN

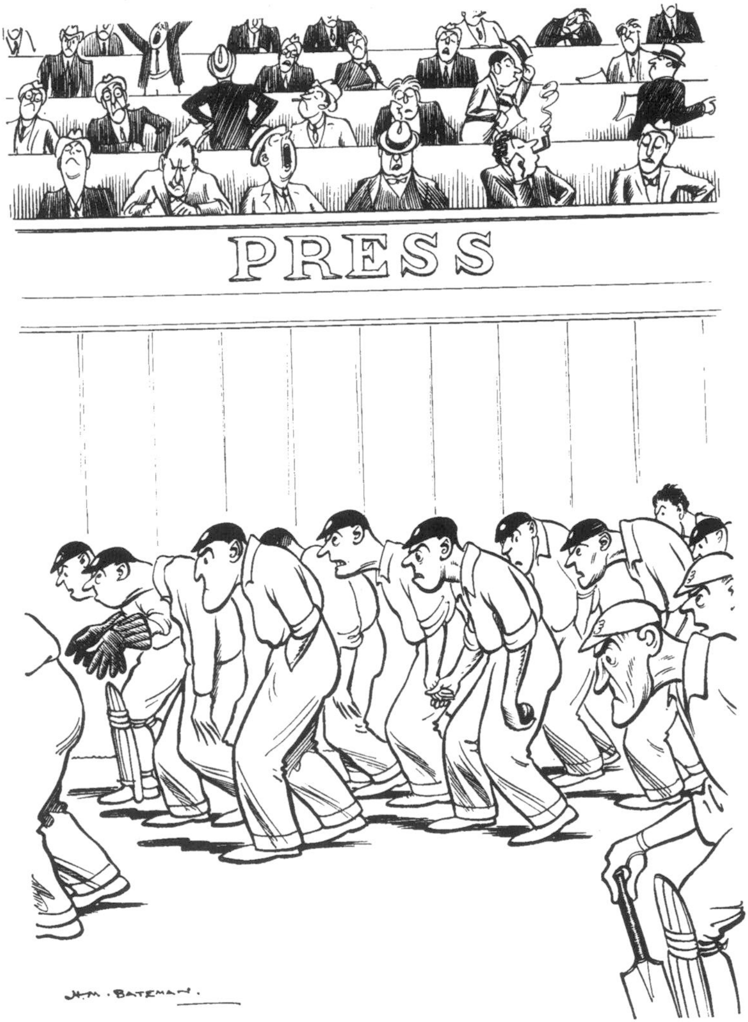
PRESS
H.M. BATEMAN.

The Cricket Match That Did Not Produce a Record

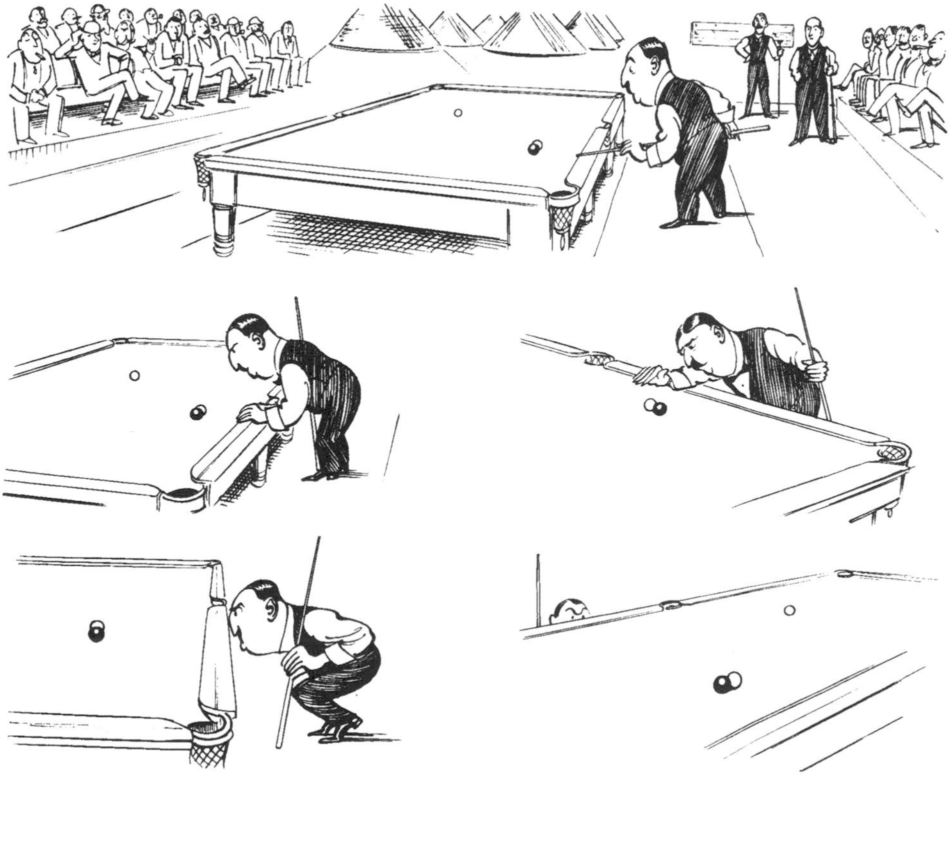

Were They Touching?

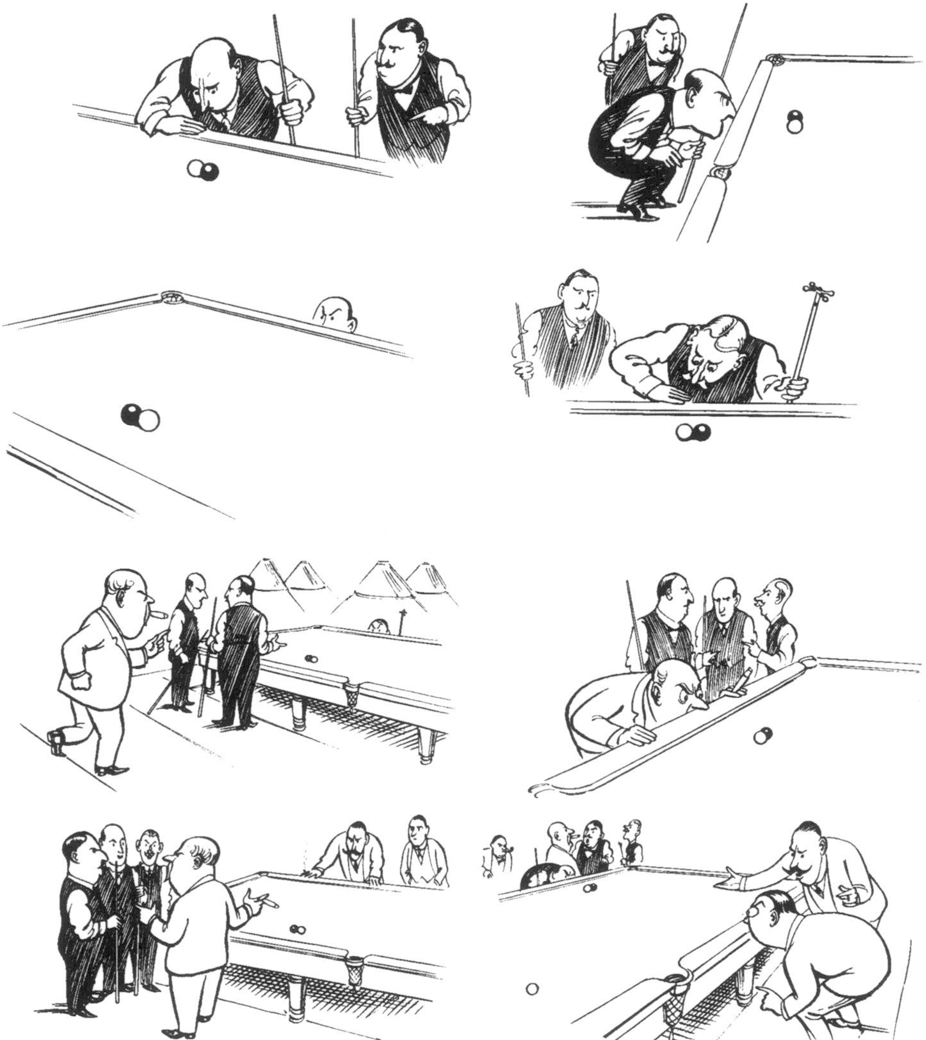

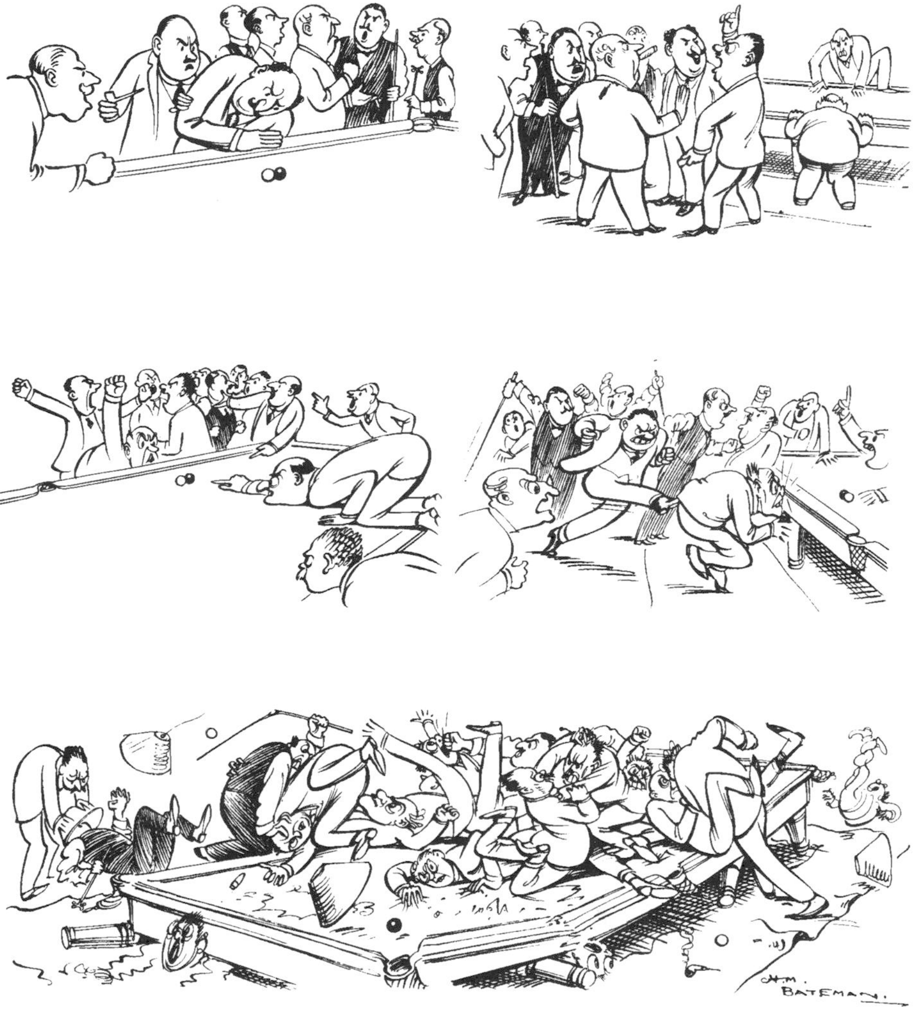
H.M. BATEMAN.

It's All in the Game

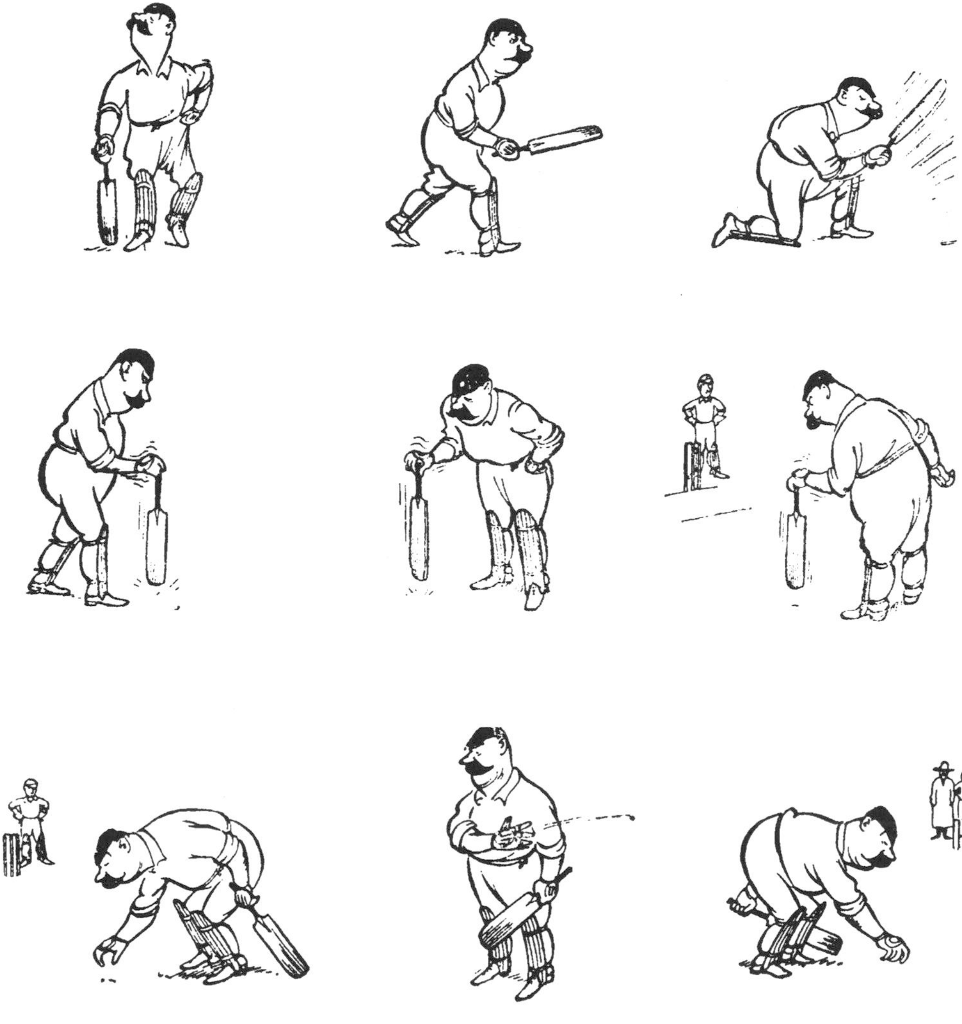

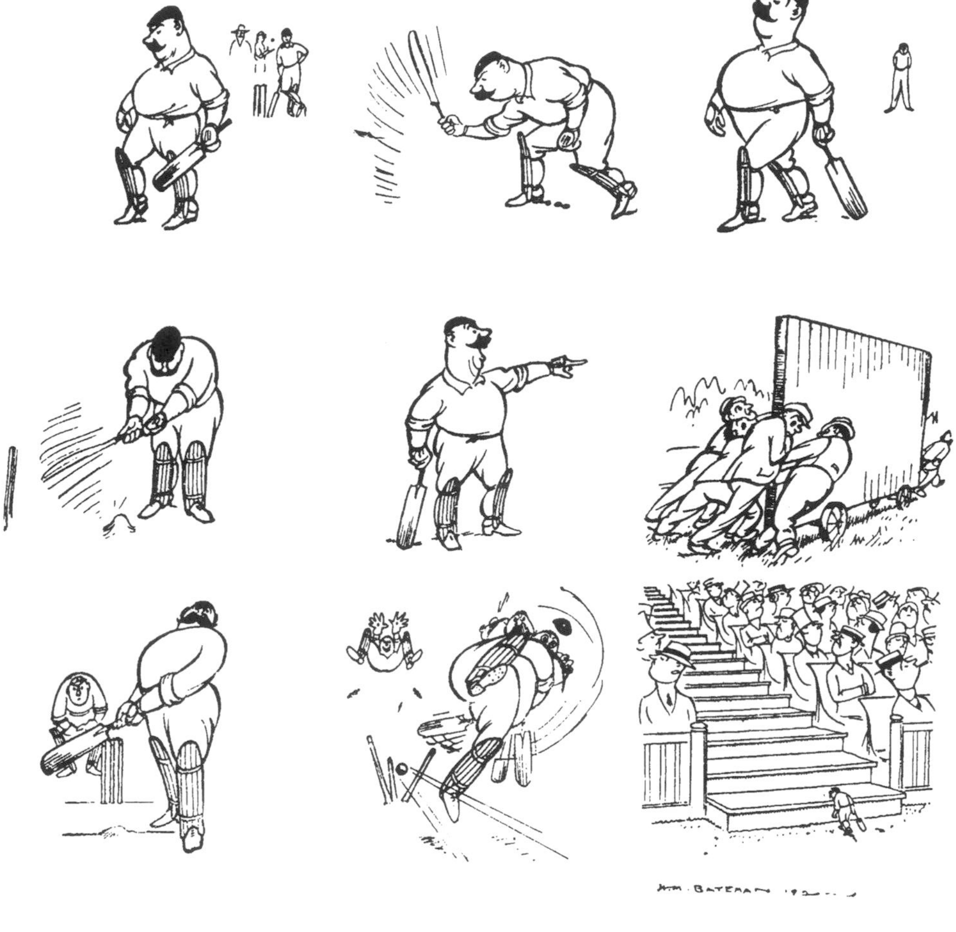
H.M. BATEMAN

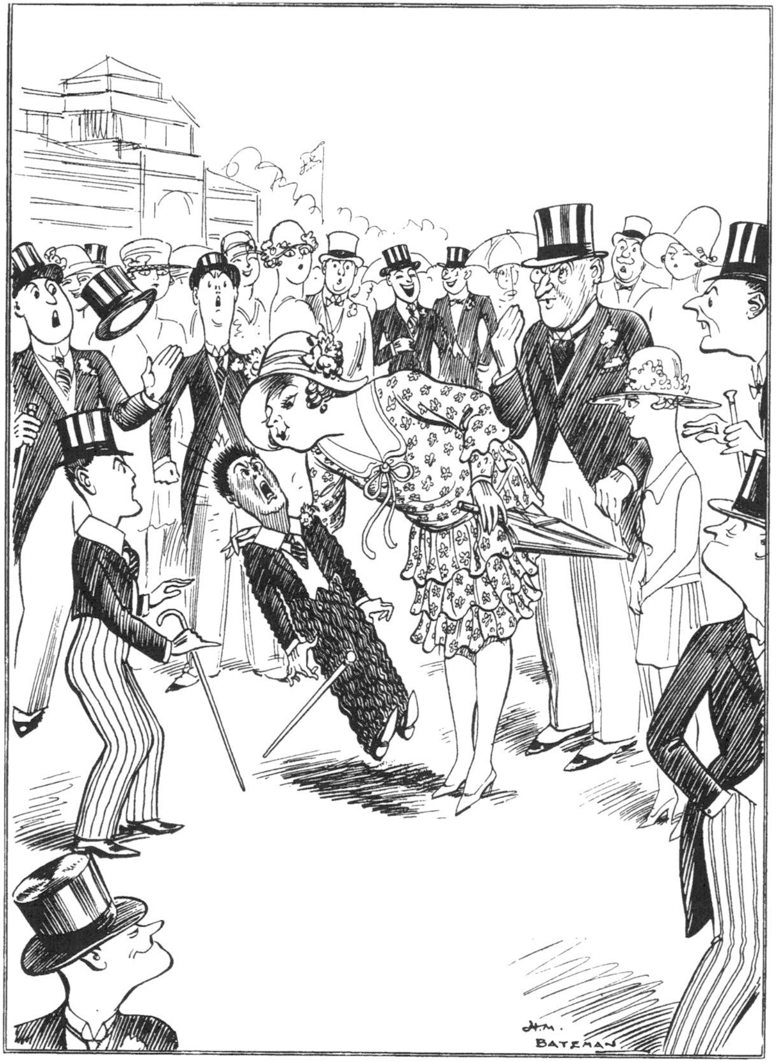
H.M. BATEMAN

The Mother Who Kissed Her Son at Lord's

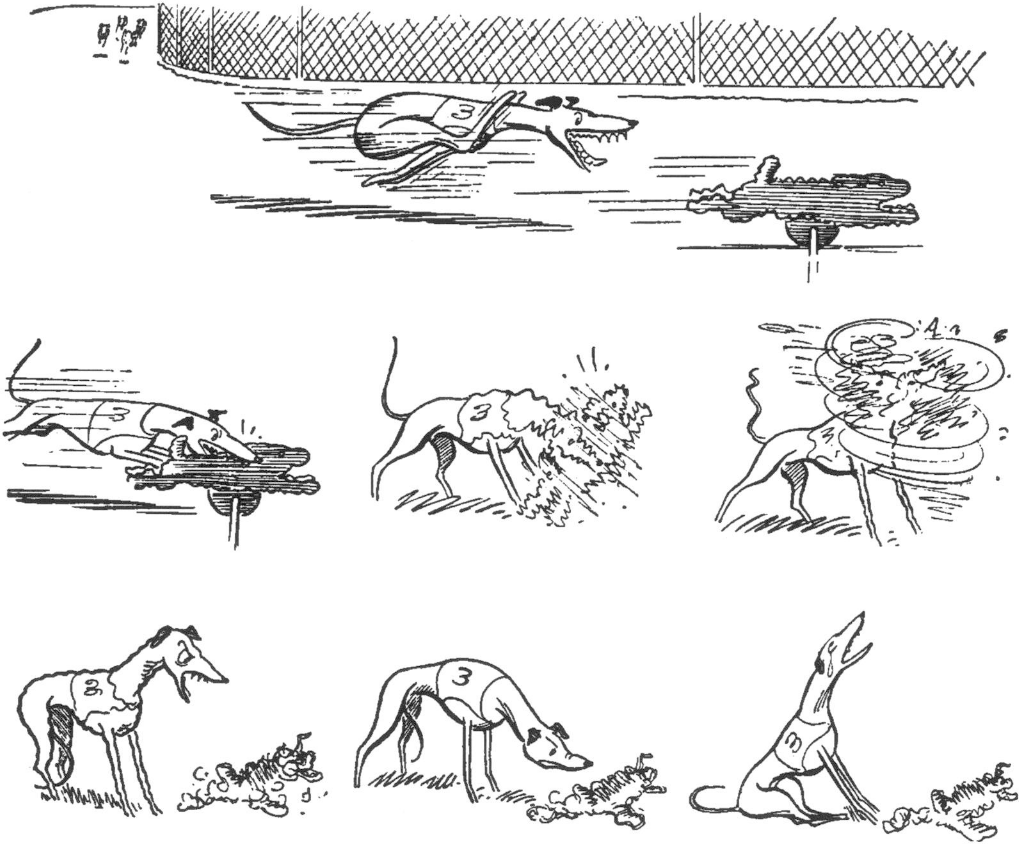

The Dog That Caught It

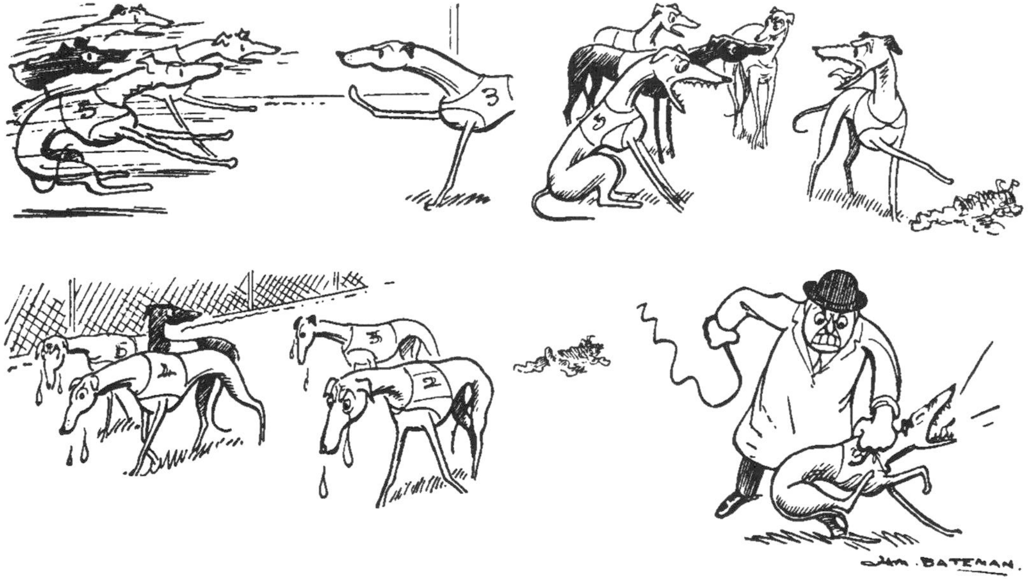
H.M. BATEMAN.

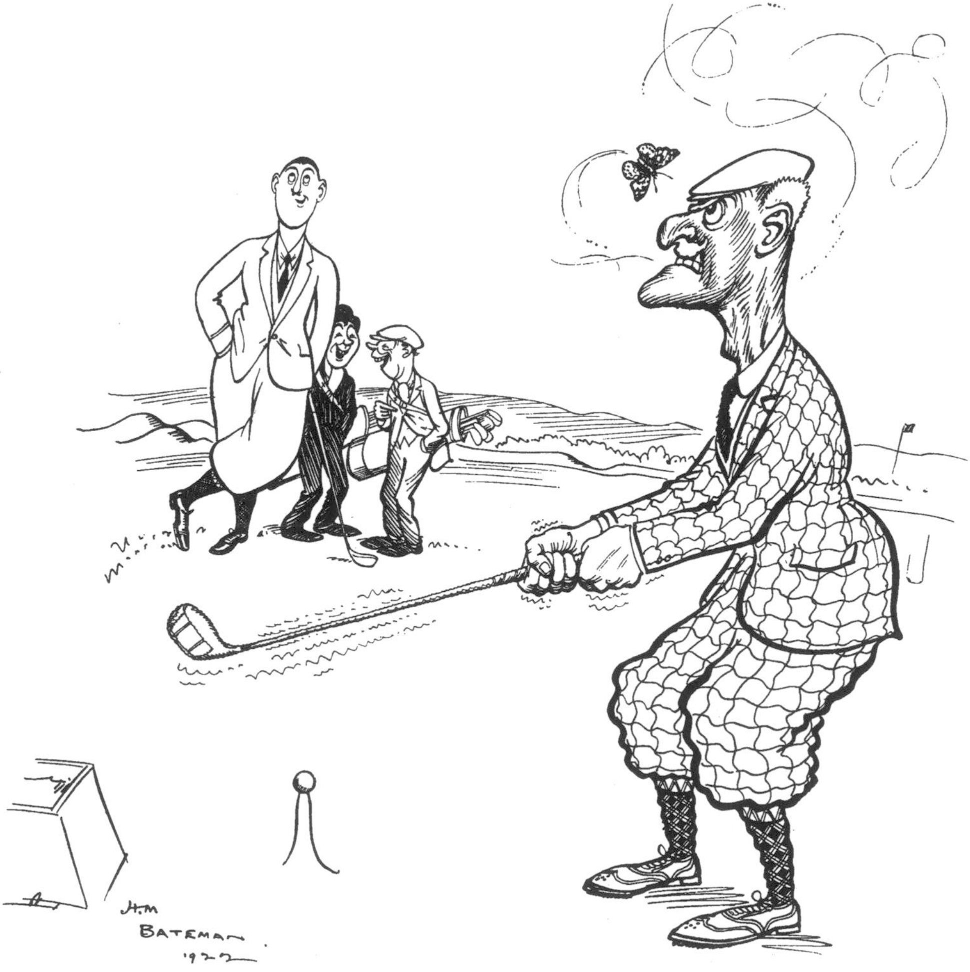
H.M
BATEMAN

The Colonel and the Painted Lady

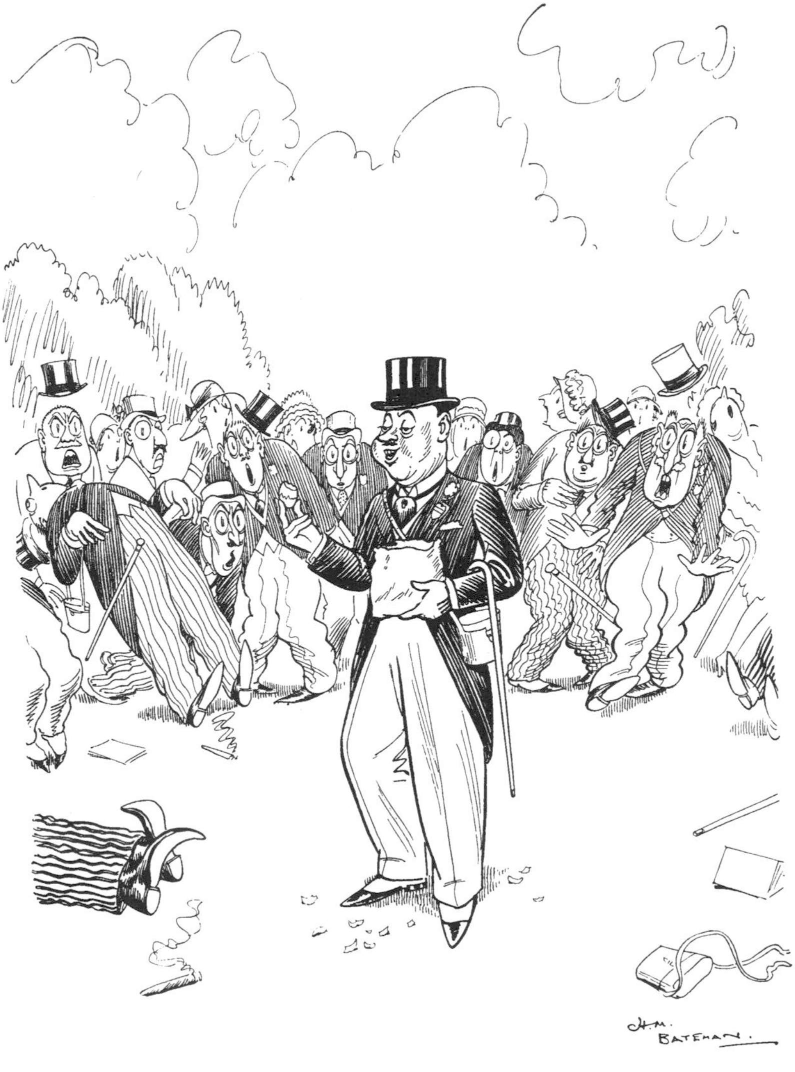
H.M. BATEMAN.

The Man Who Ate His Luncheon in the Royal Enclosure

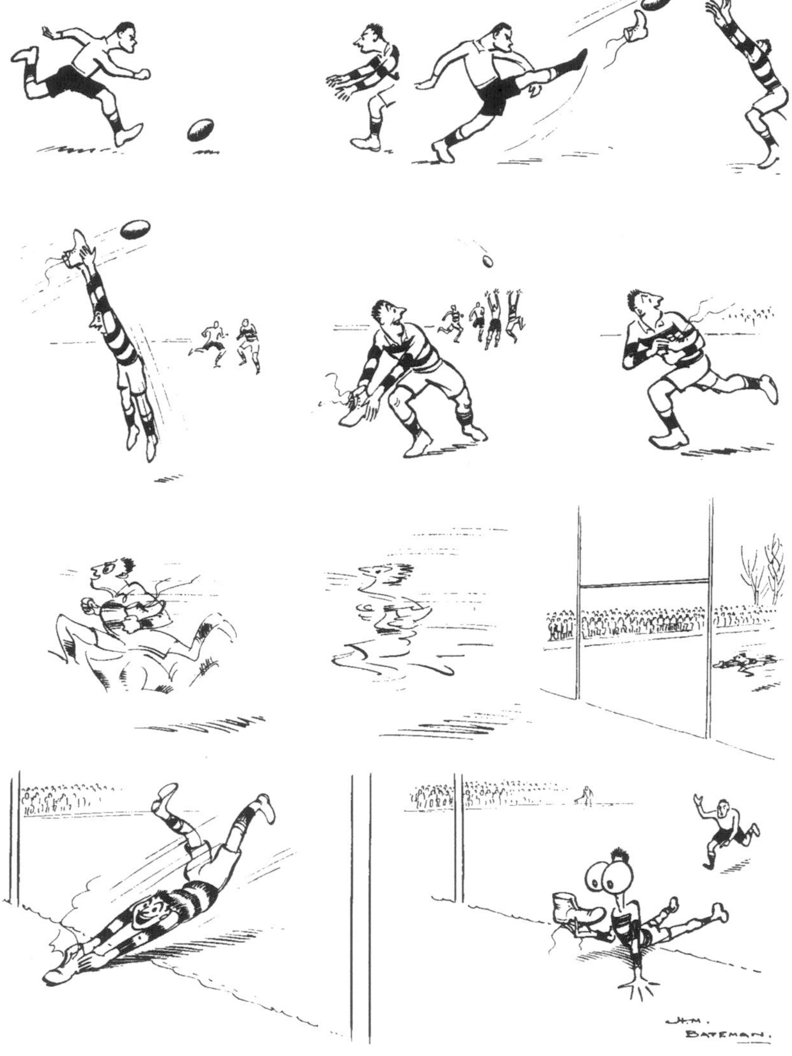
H.M. BATEMAN.

A Wasted Effort

The Social Sphere

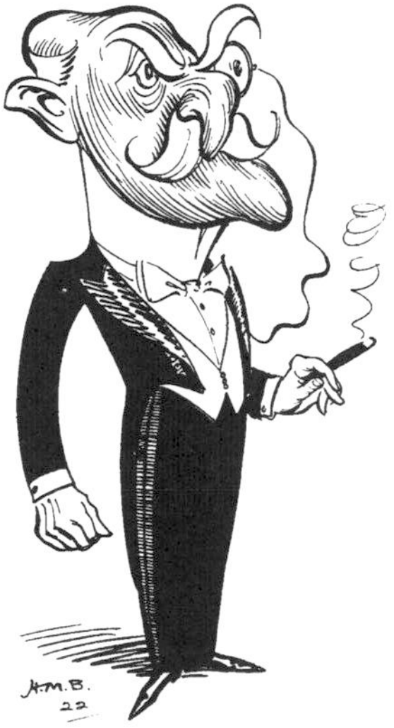
H.M.B.
22

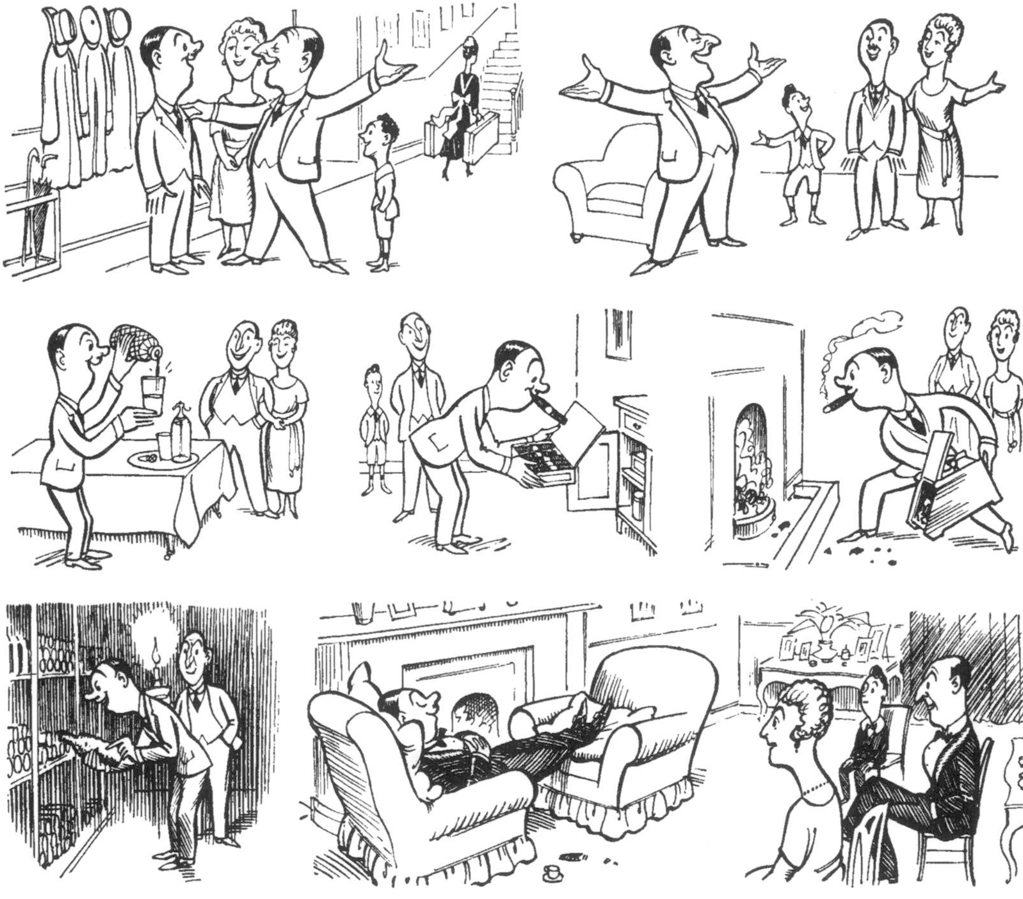

The Guest Who Was Told to Make Himself
Quite at Home, and Did So

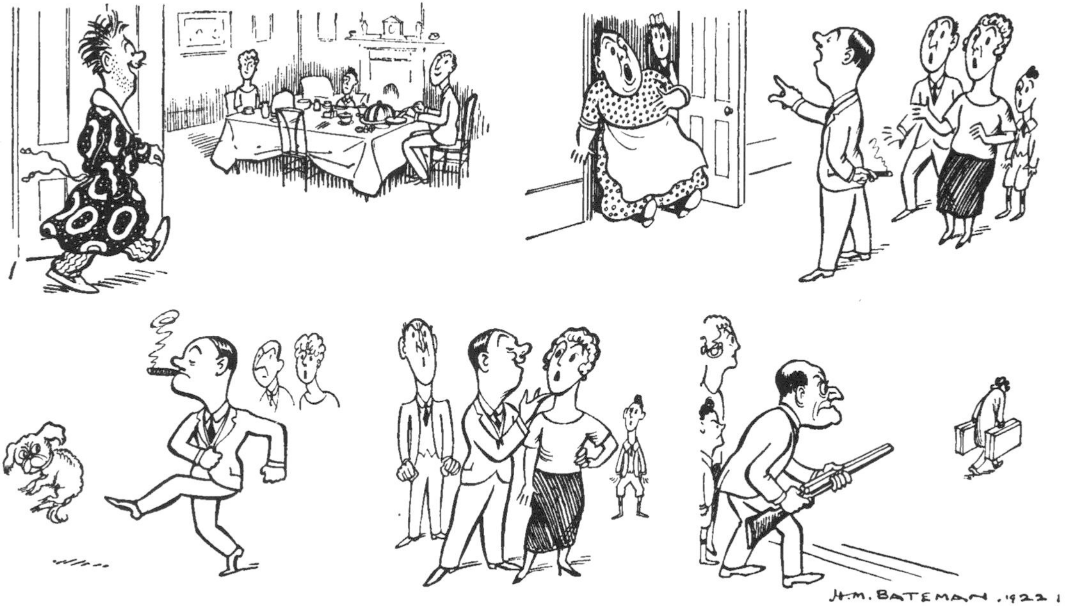
H.M. BATEMAN. 1922.

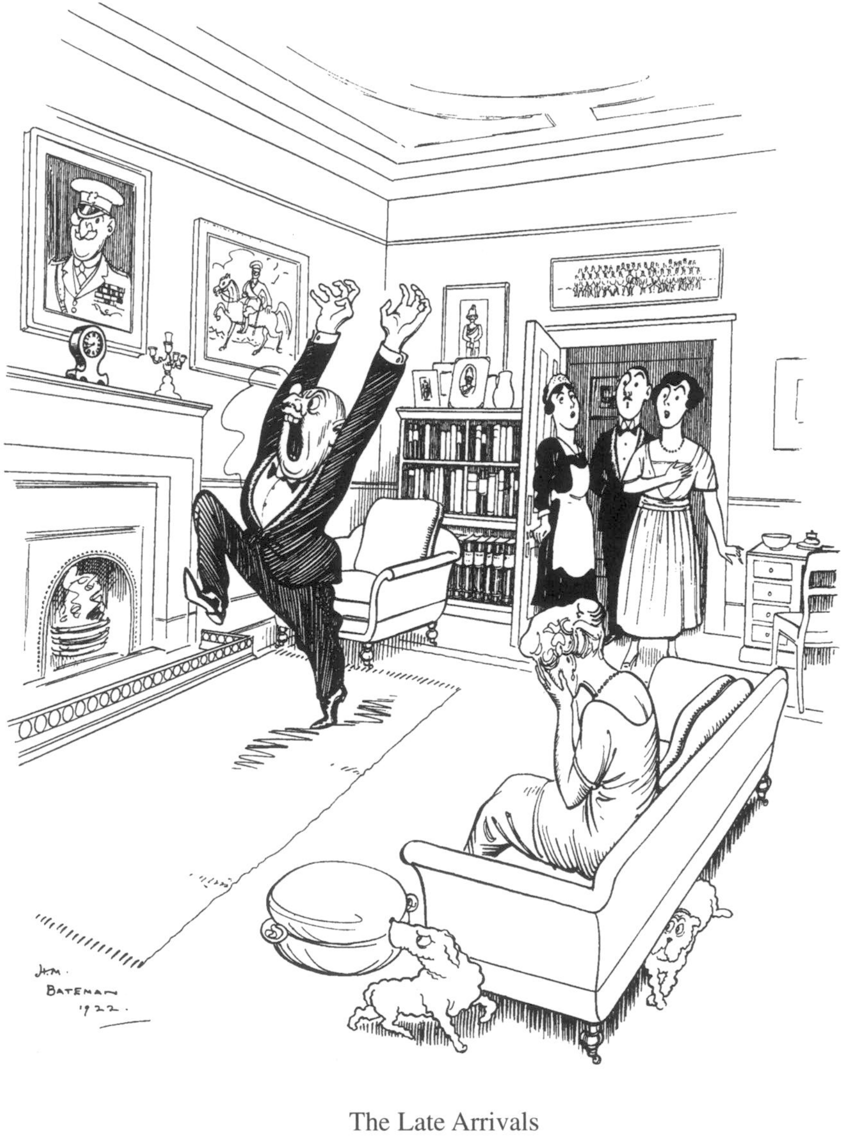
H.M. BATEMAN 1922.

The Late Arrivals

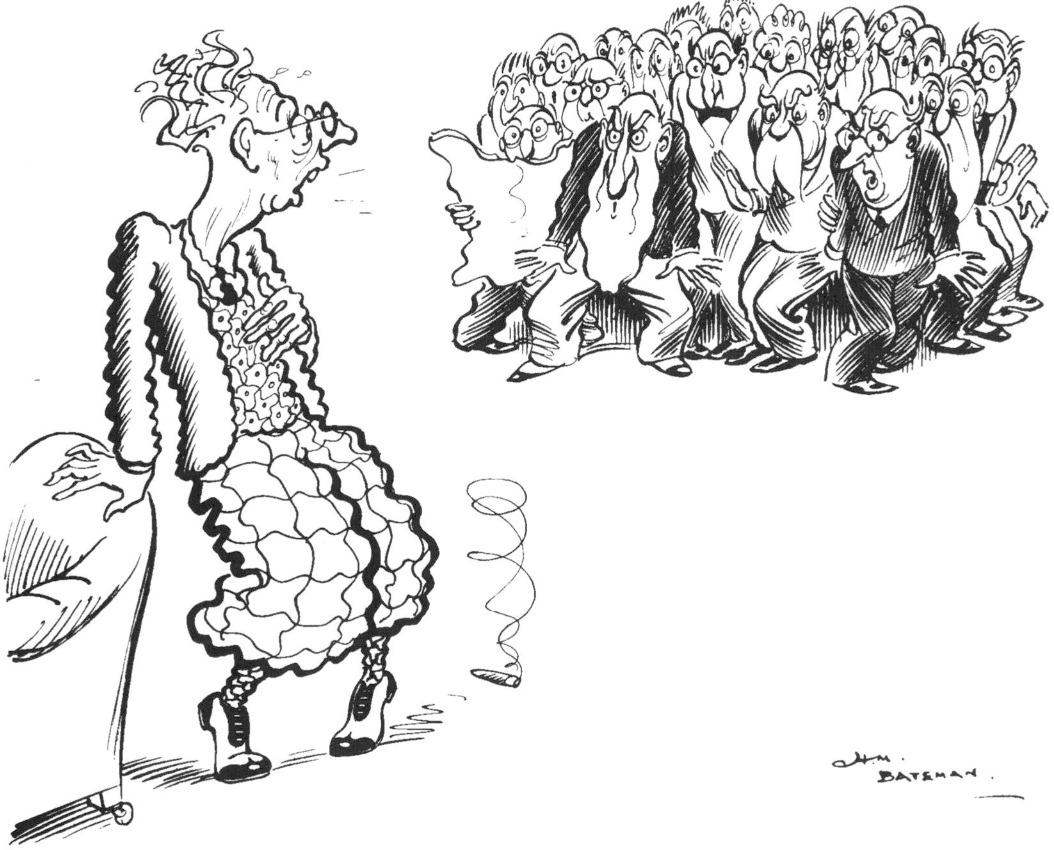
H.M. BATEMAN.

A Member of the Athenaeum Attempts Plus-Fours

The Man Who Will Not Share the Fire

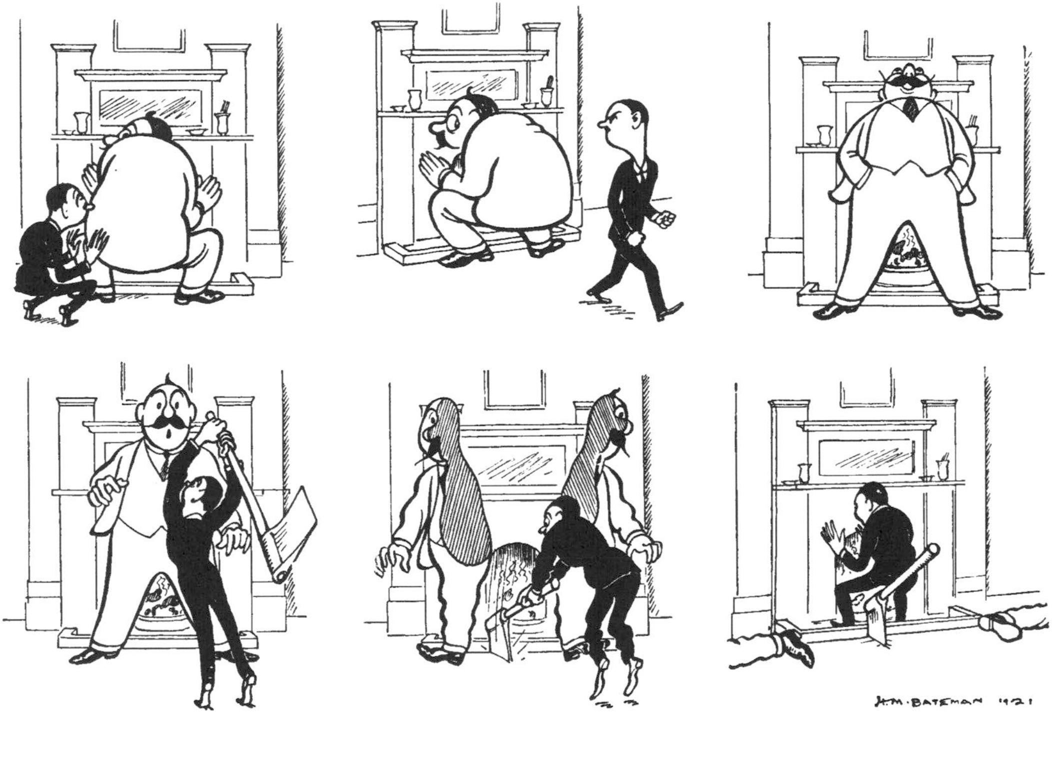
H.M. BATEMAN 1921

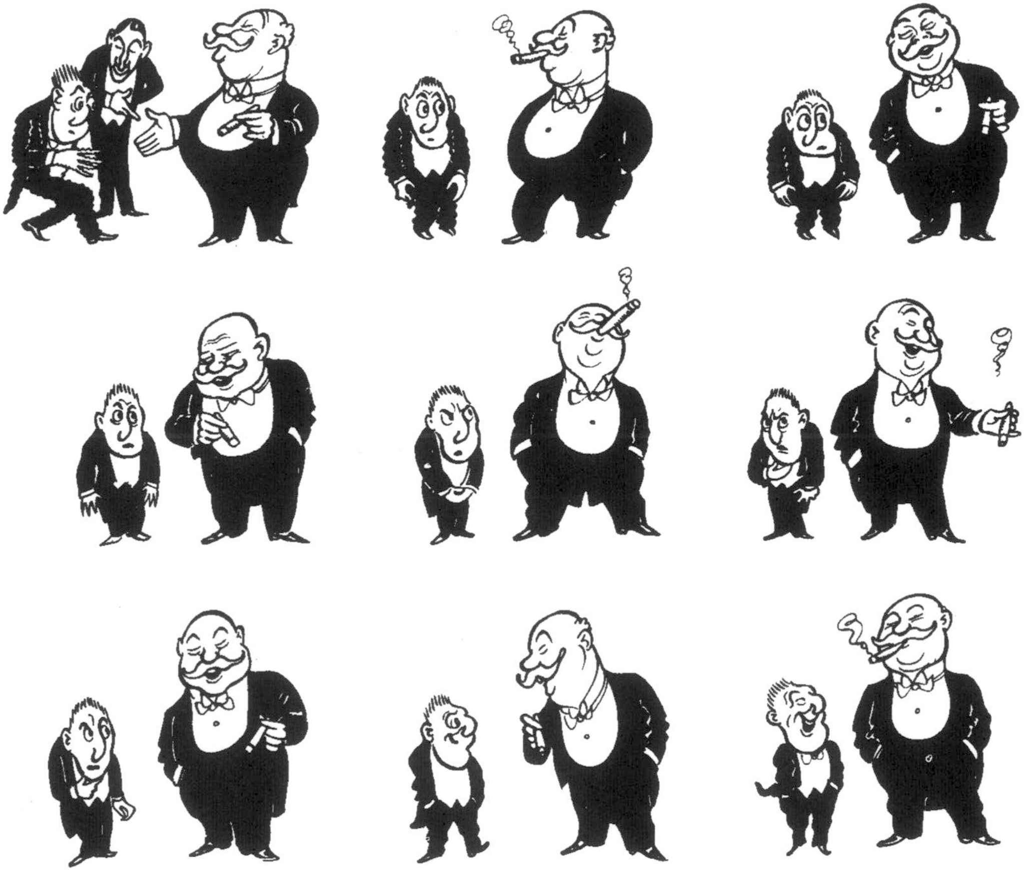

Familiarity Breeds Contempt

HM. BATEMAN 1920.

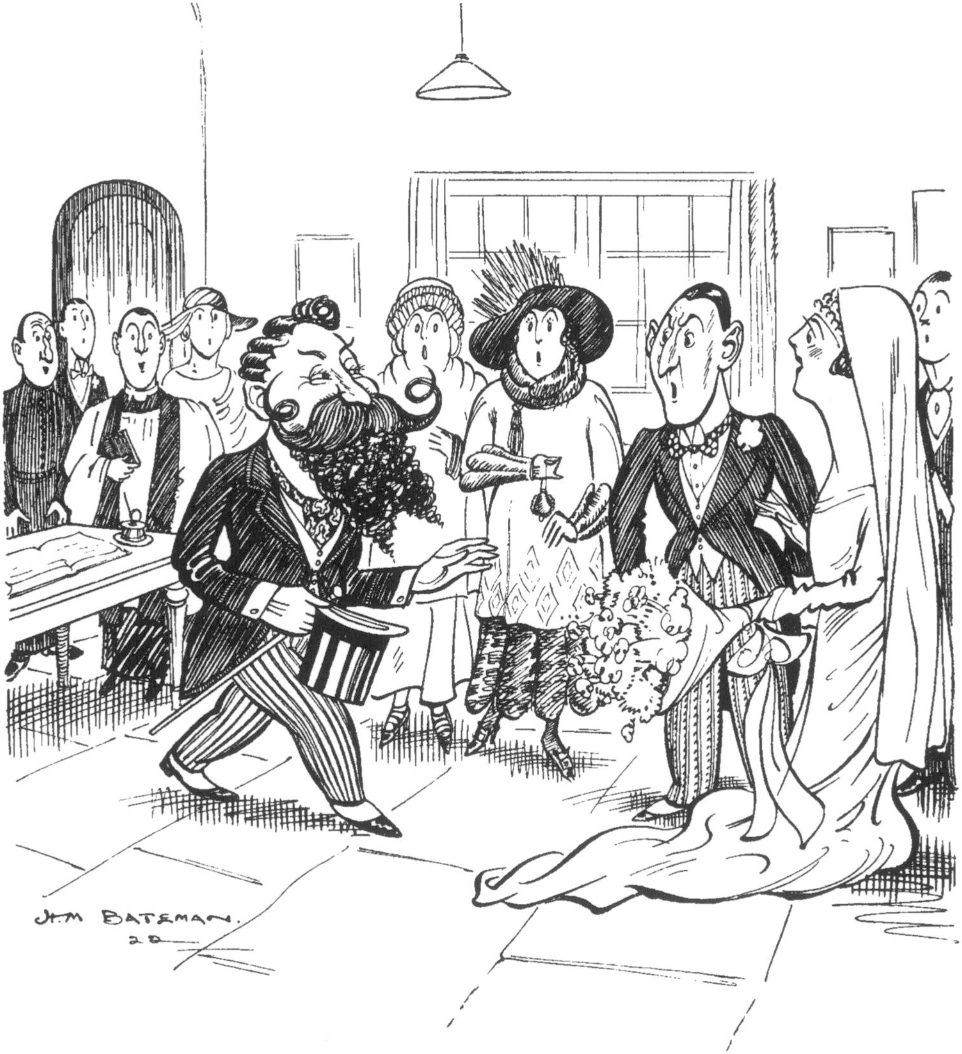
H.M. BATEMAN.
22

The Guest Who Wanted to Kiss the Bride

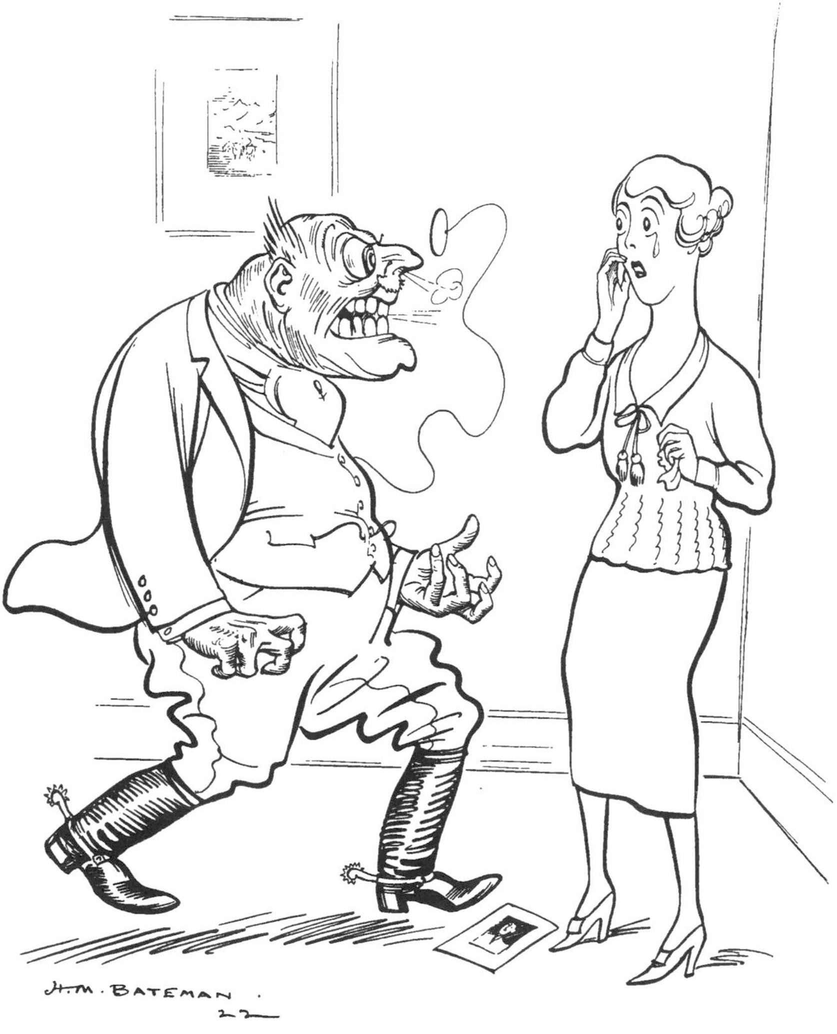
H.M. BATEMAN
22

The Colonel Implores His Daughter to be Reasonable

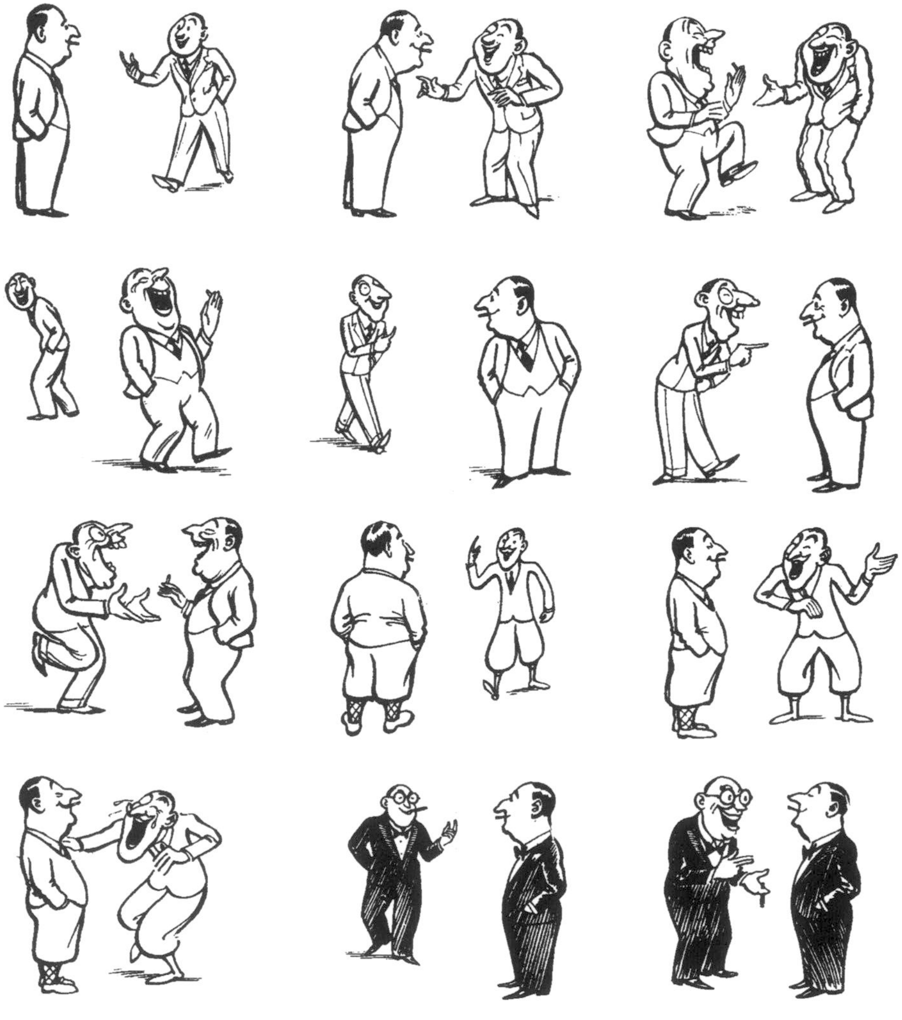

The Funny Story, or Too Much of a Good Thing

SHOOTEM &
GUNSMIT
H.M. BATEMAN

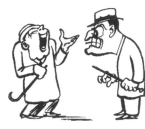

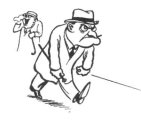

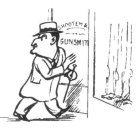

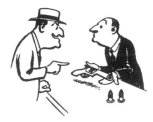

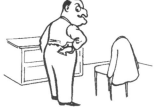

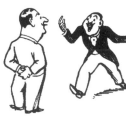

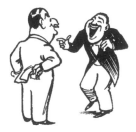

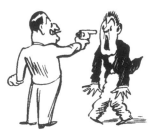

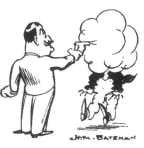

A Colourful Mixture

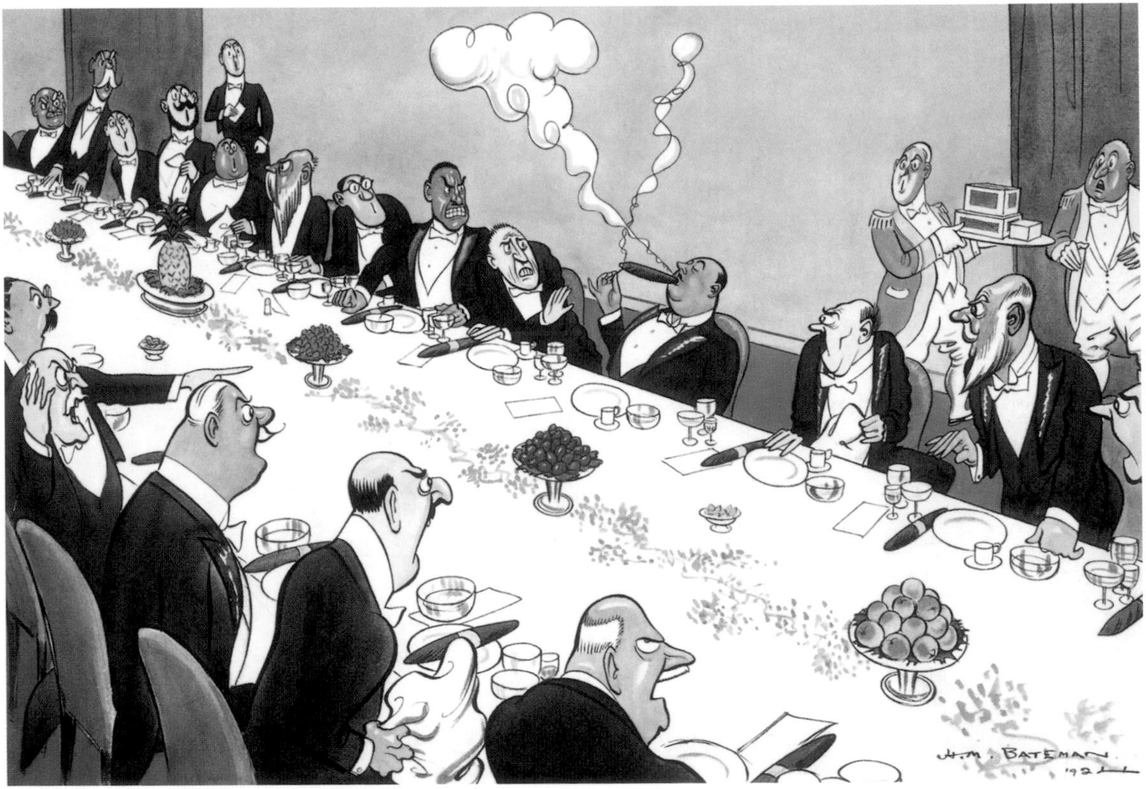
H.M. BATEMAN.

The Man Who Lit His Cigar Before the Loyal Toast

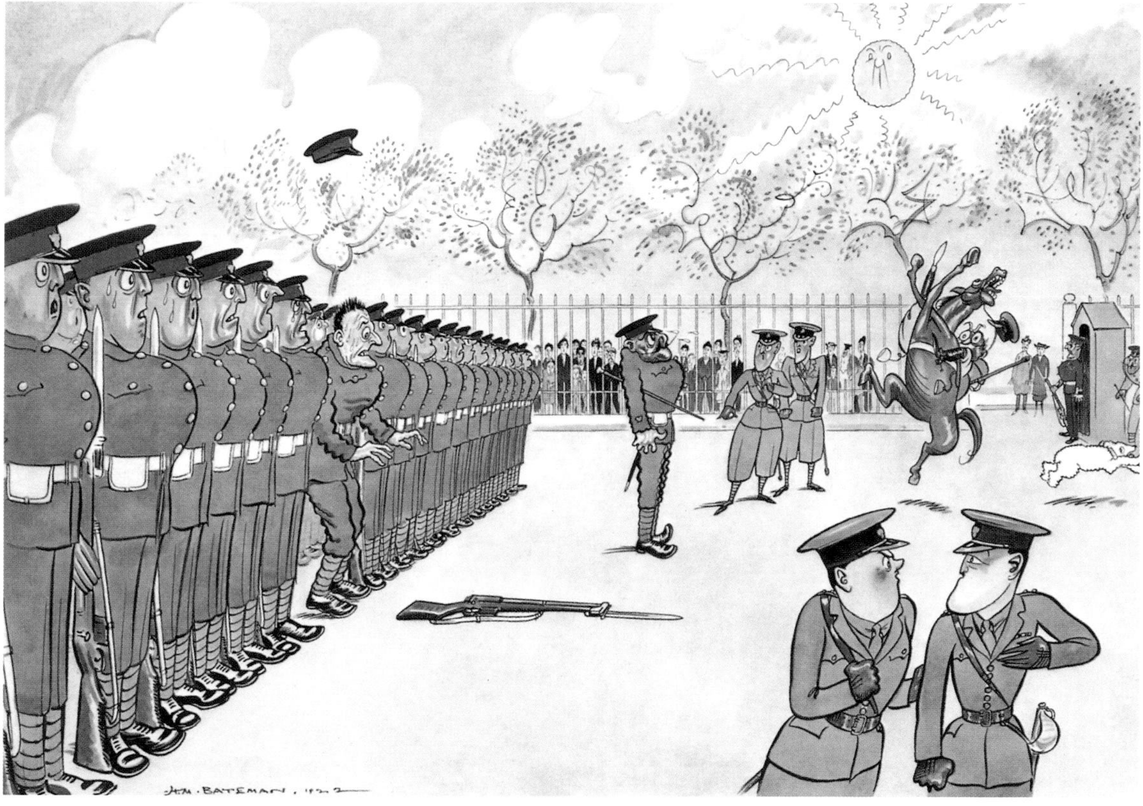
H.M. BATEMAN . 1922

The Guardsman Who Dropped It

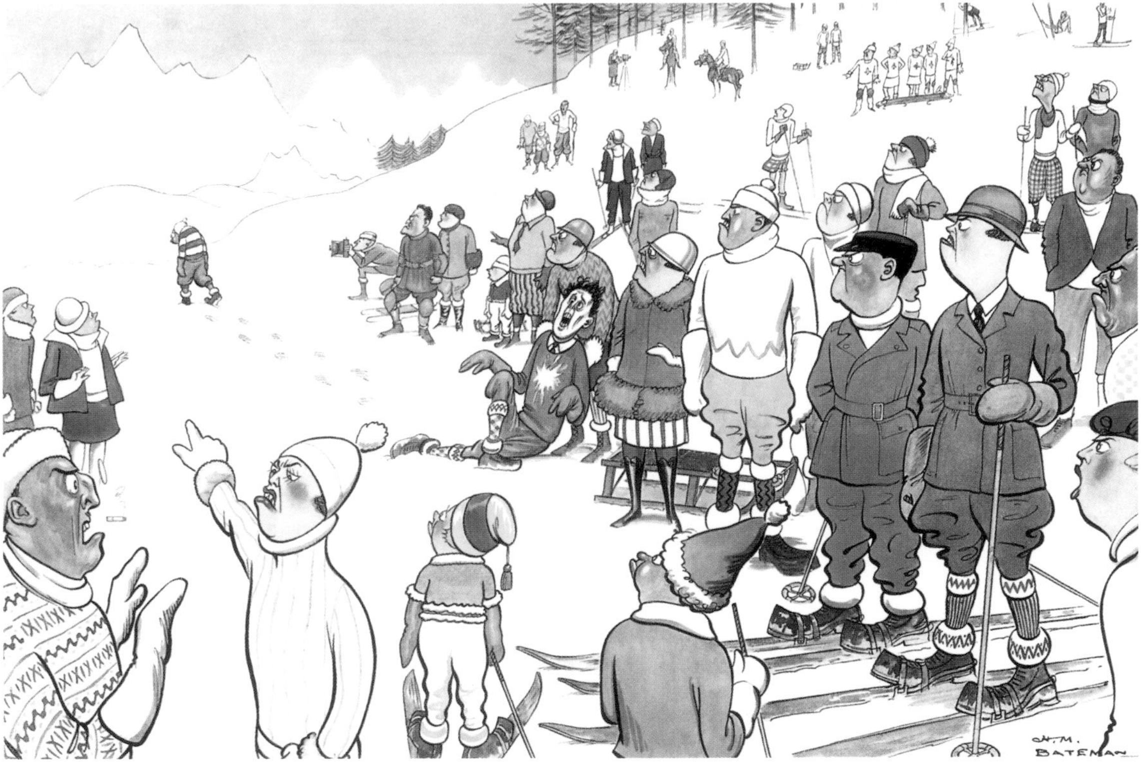
H.M. BATEMAN

The Man Who Threw a Snowball at St Moritz

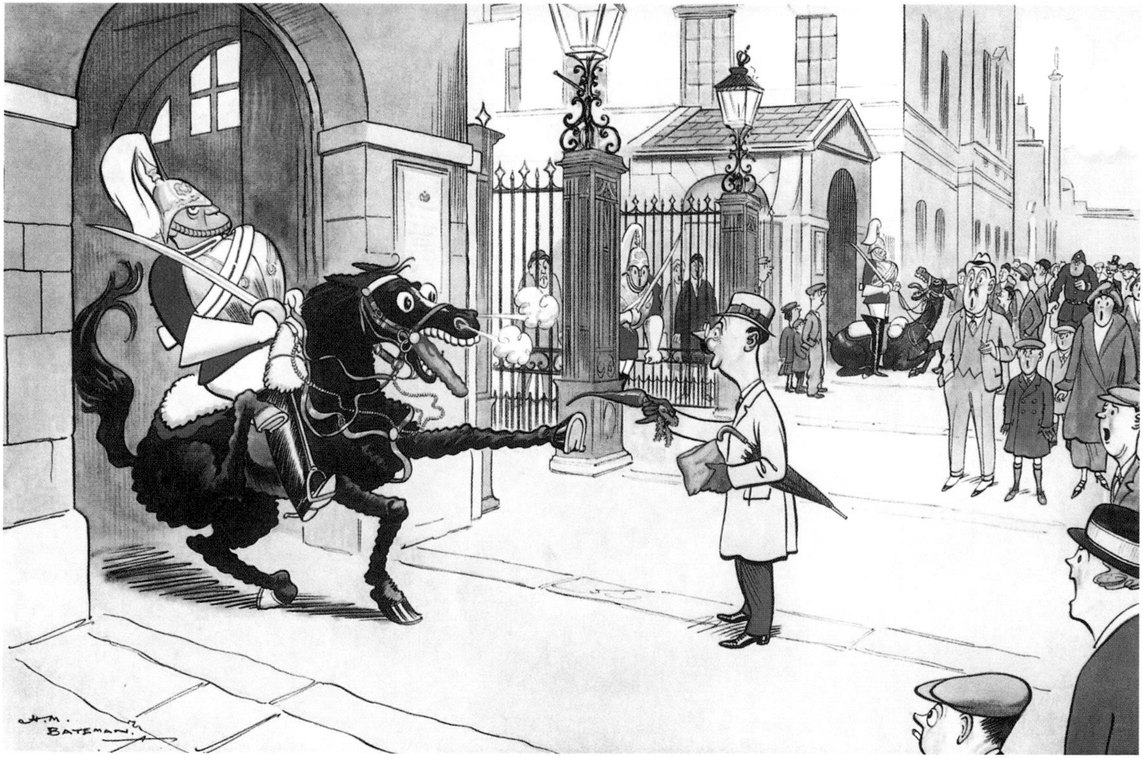
H.M. BATEMAN.

Very Well Meant

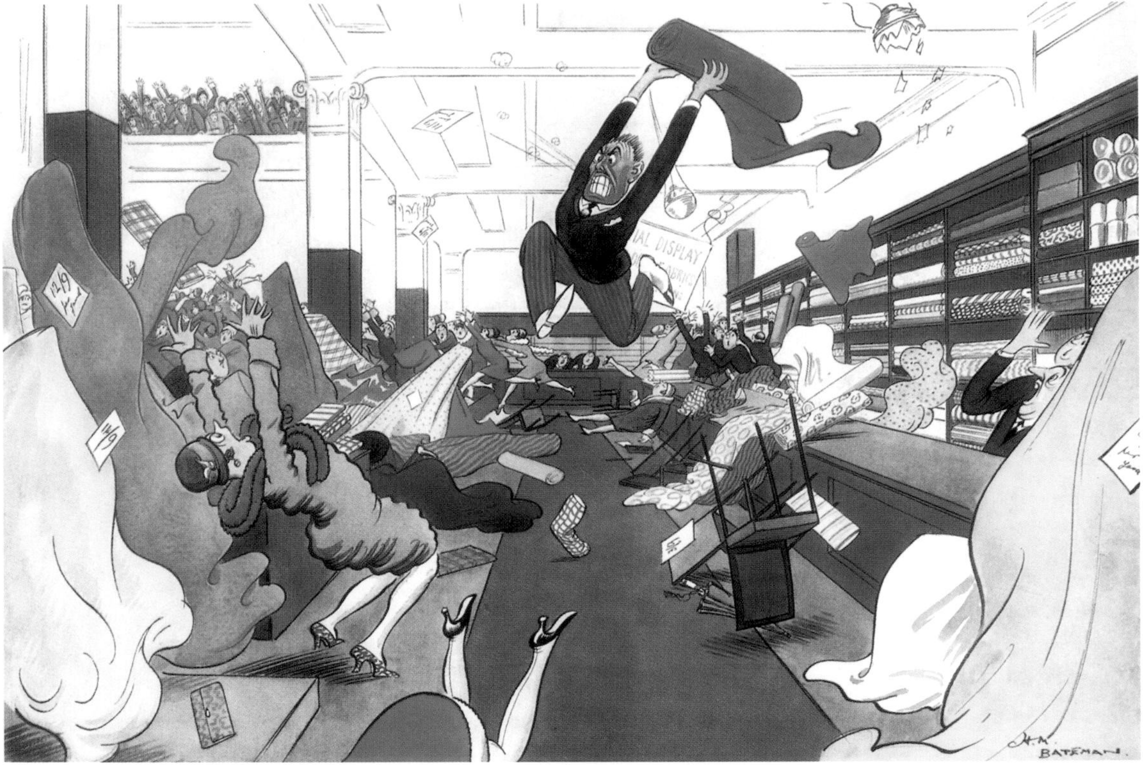
H.M. BATEMAN.

The Shop Assistant Who Lost His Temper

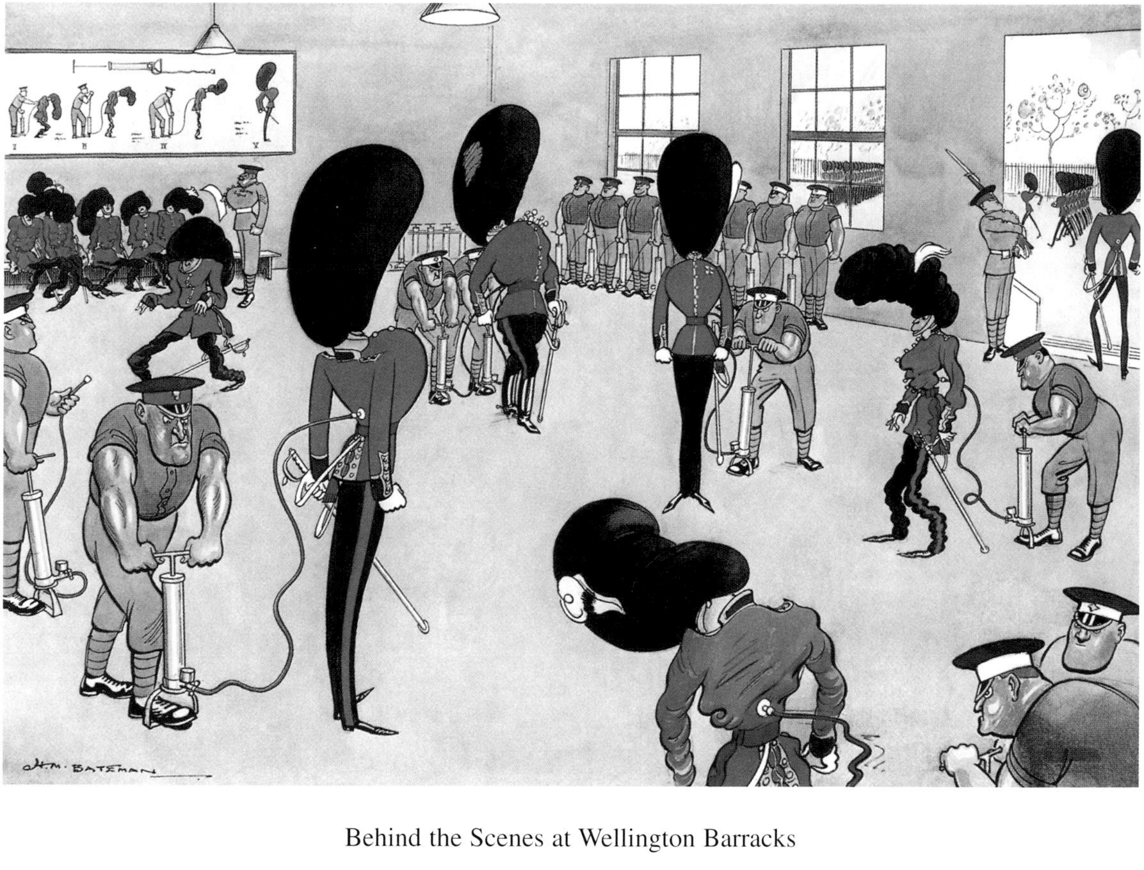
H.M. BATEMAN

Behind the Scenes at Wellington Barracks

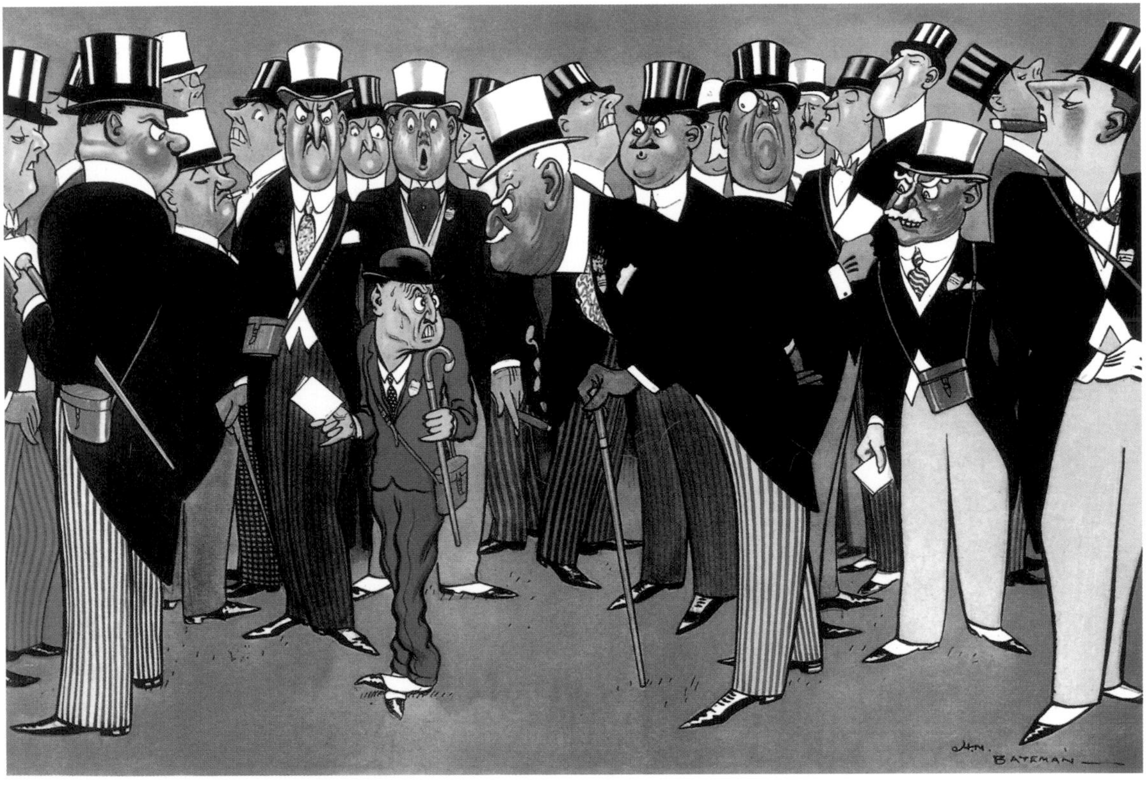
H.M. BATEMAN

The Man Who Crept into the Royal Enclosure in a Bowler

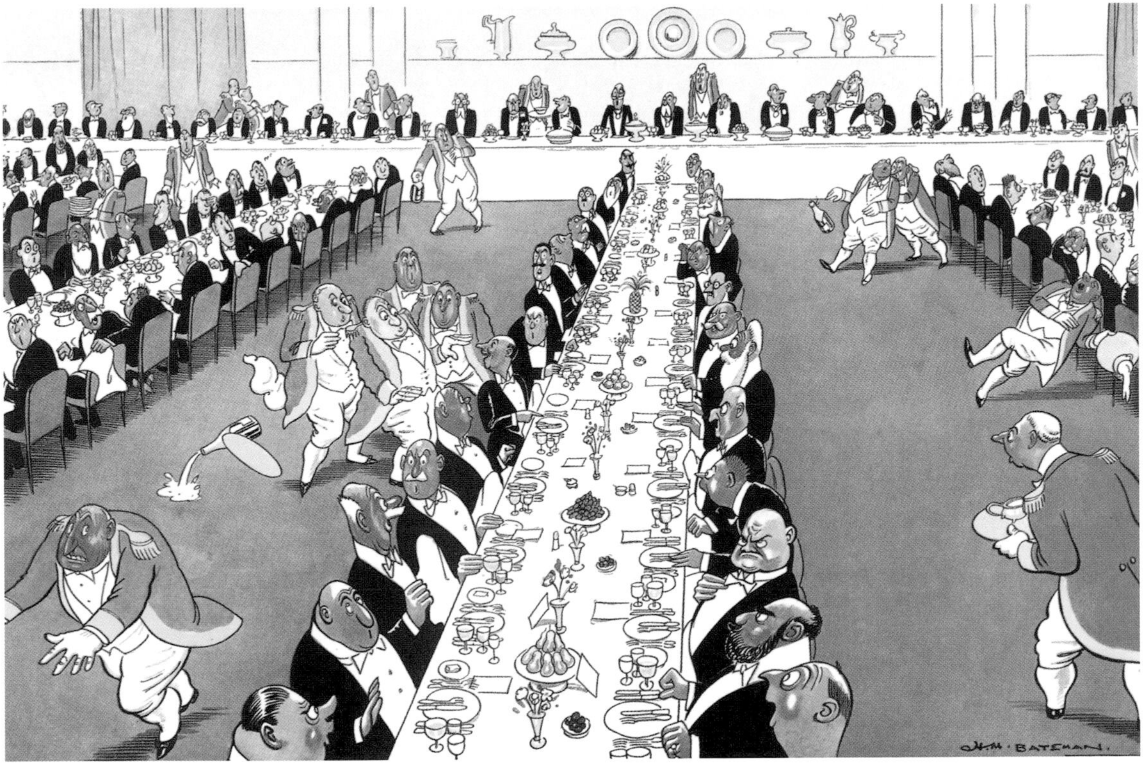
H.M. BATEMAN.

The Man Asked For a Second Helping at a City Company Dinner

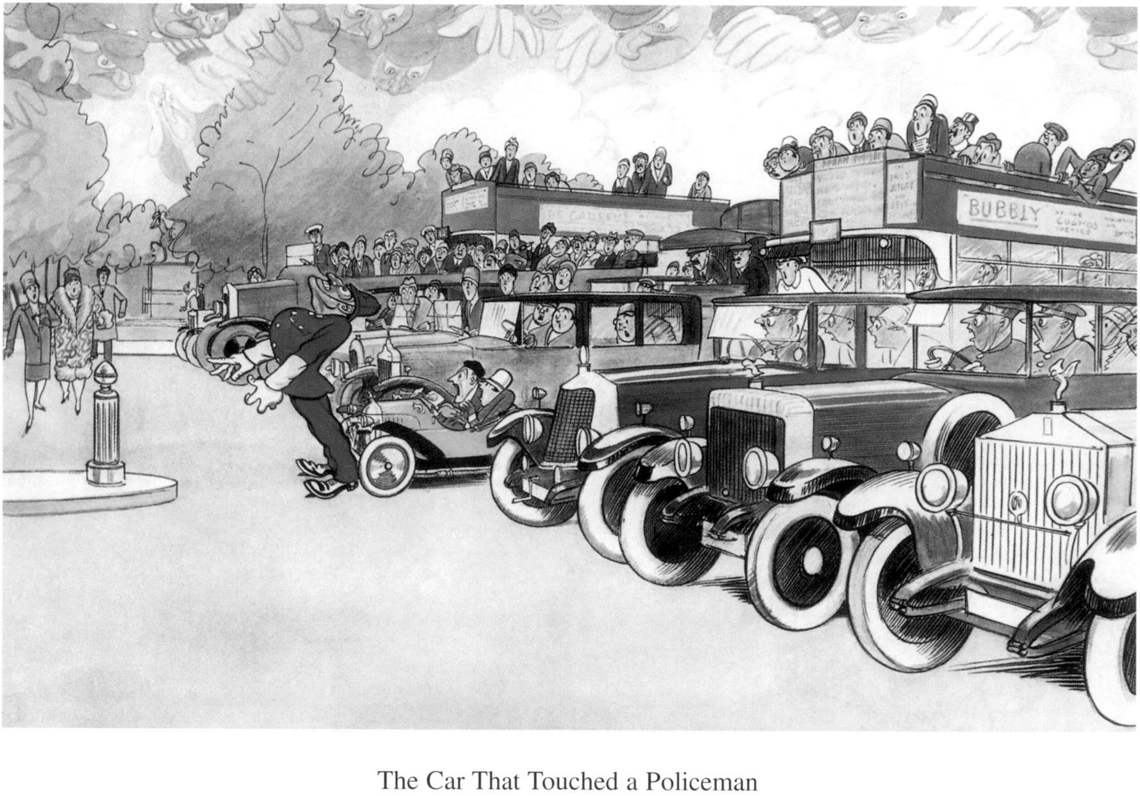
BUBBLY

The Car That Touched a Policeman

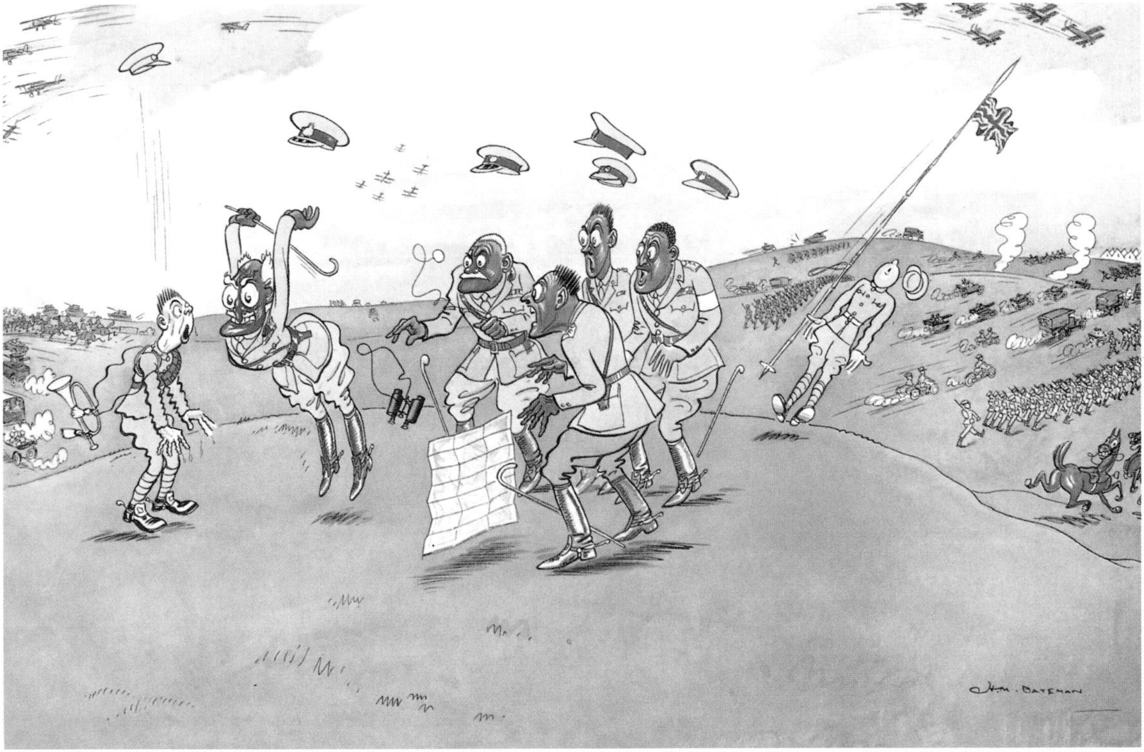
H.M. BATEMAN

The Commander-in-Chief's Trumpeter Sounds the 'Dismiss' in Error

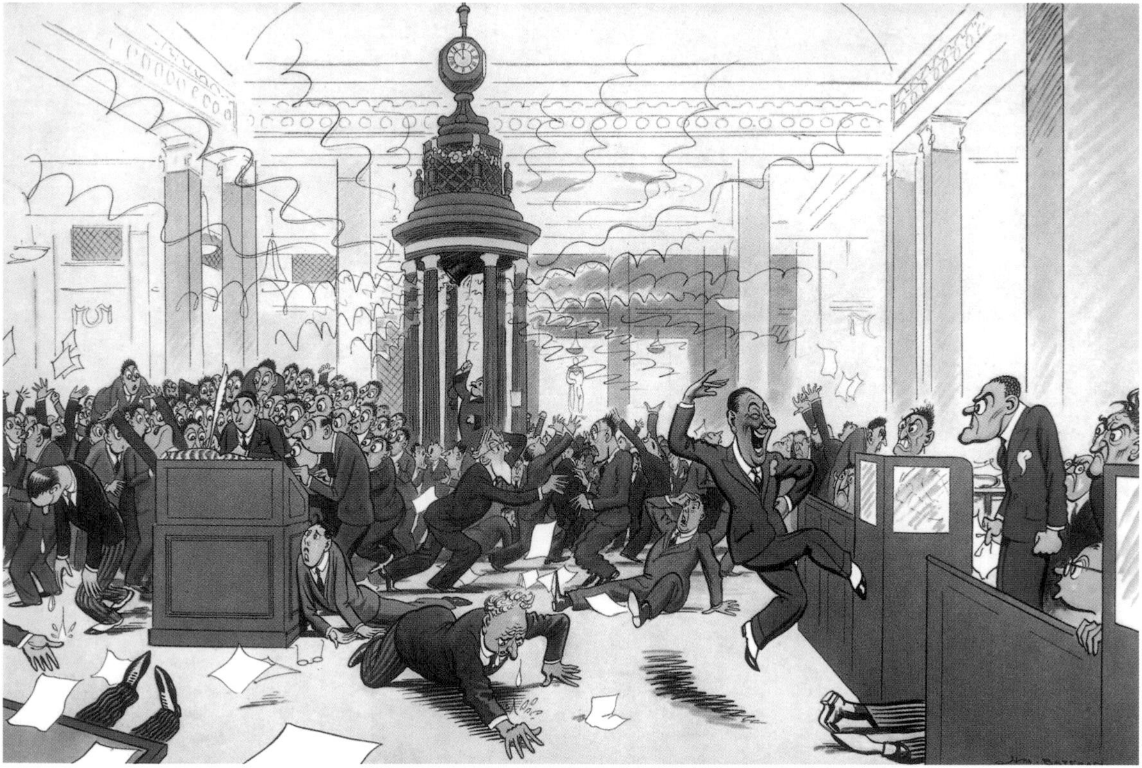

The Underwriter Who Missed a Total Loss

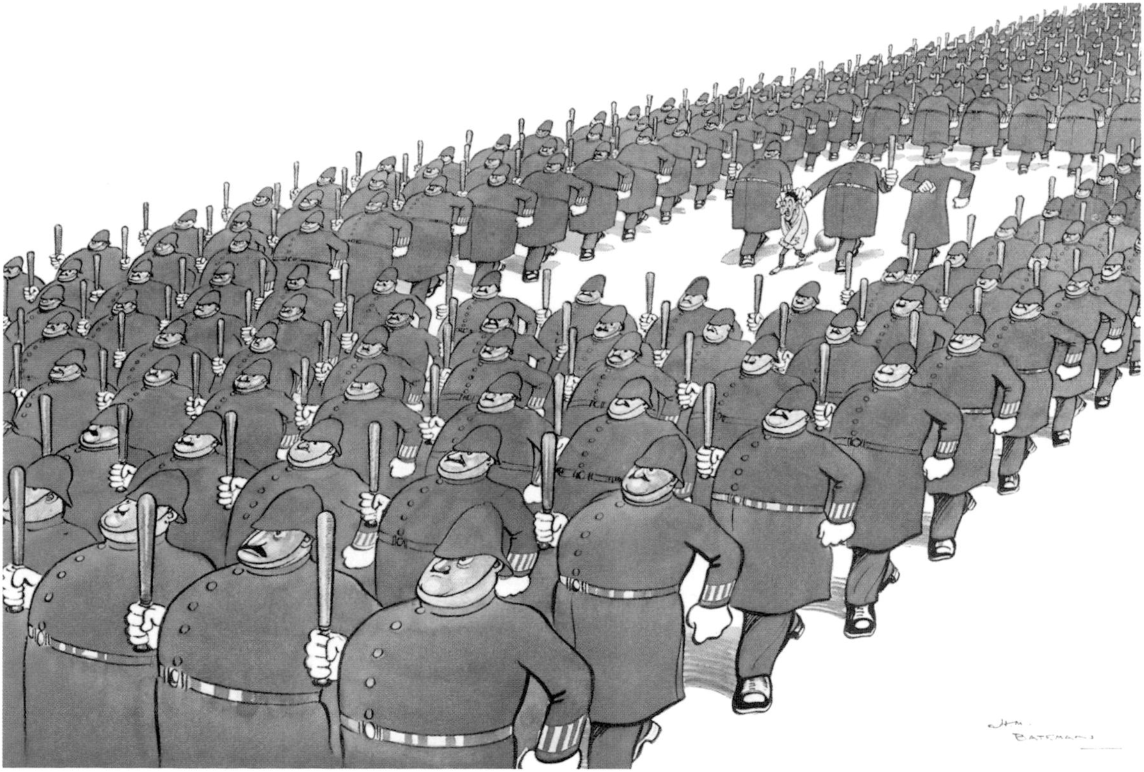

A Slight Misunderstanding With the Till

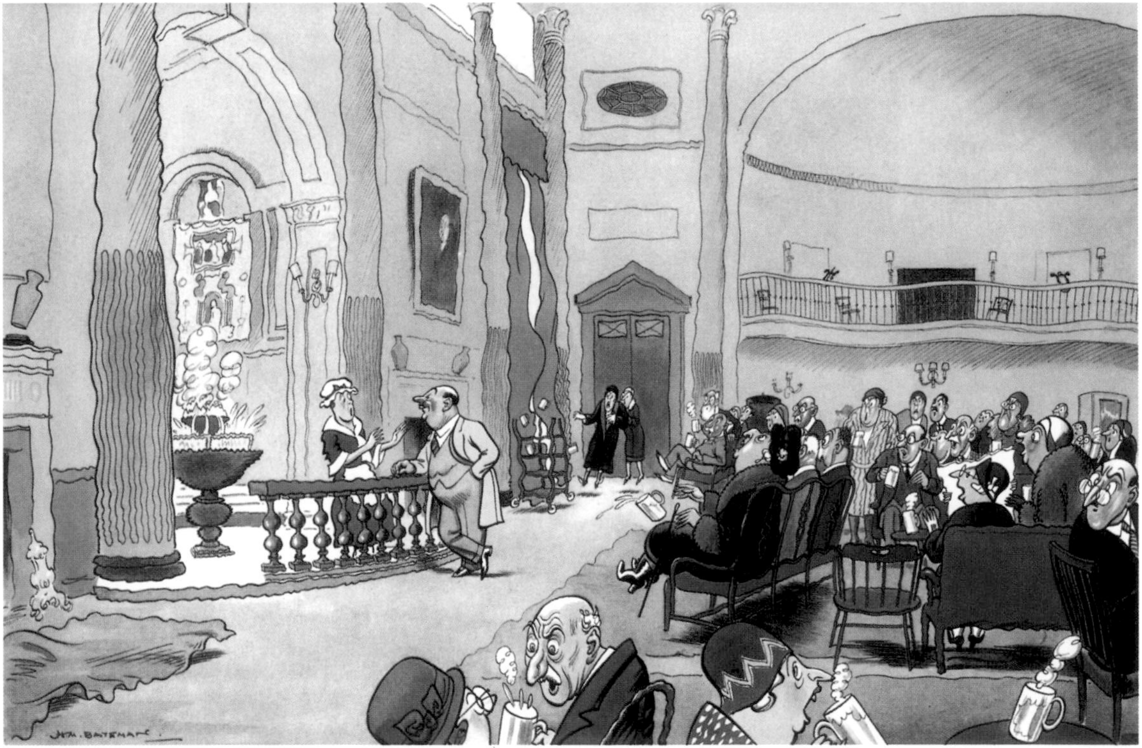
H.M. BATEMAN

The Man Who Asked For a Double Scotch in the Grand Pump Room at Bath

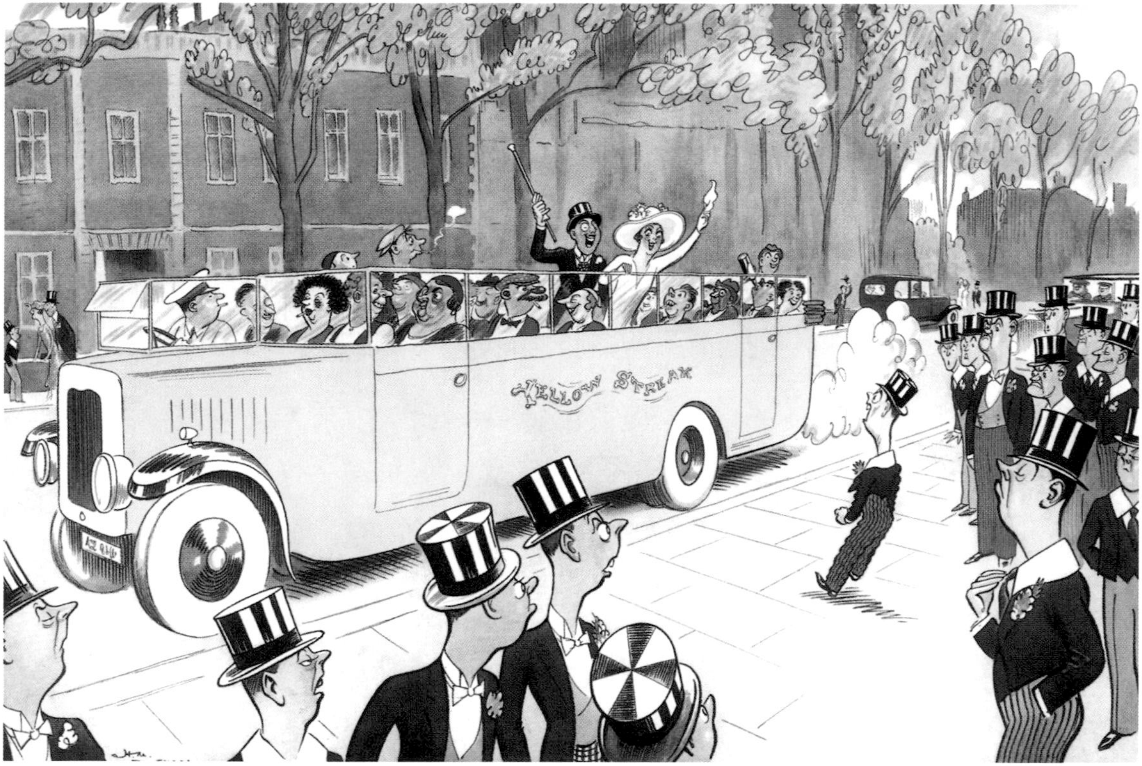
YELLOW STREAK

The Parents Who Came by Charabanc

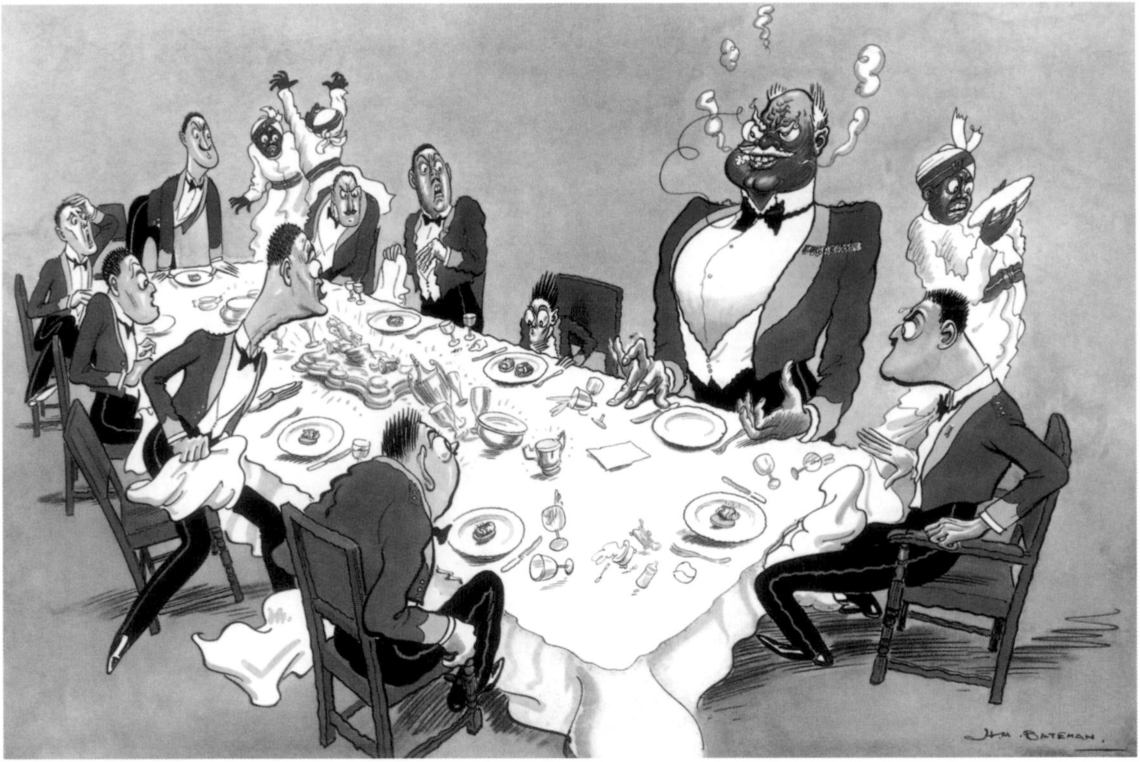
H.M. BATEMAN.

The Second Lieutenant Who Took the CO's Savoury

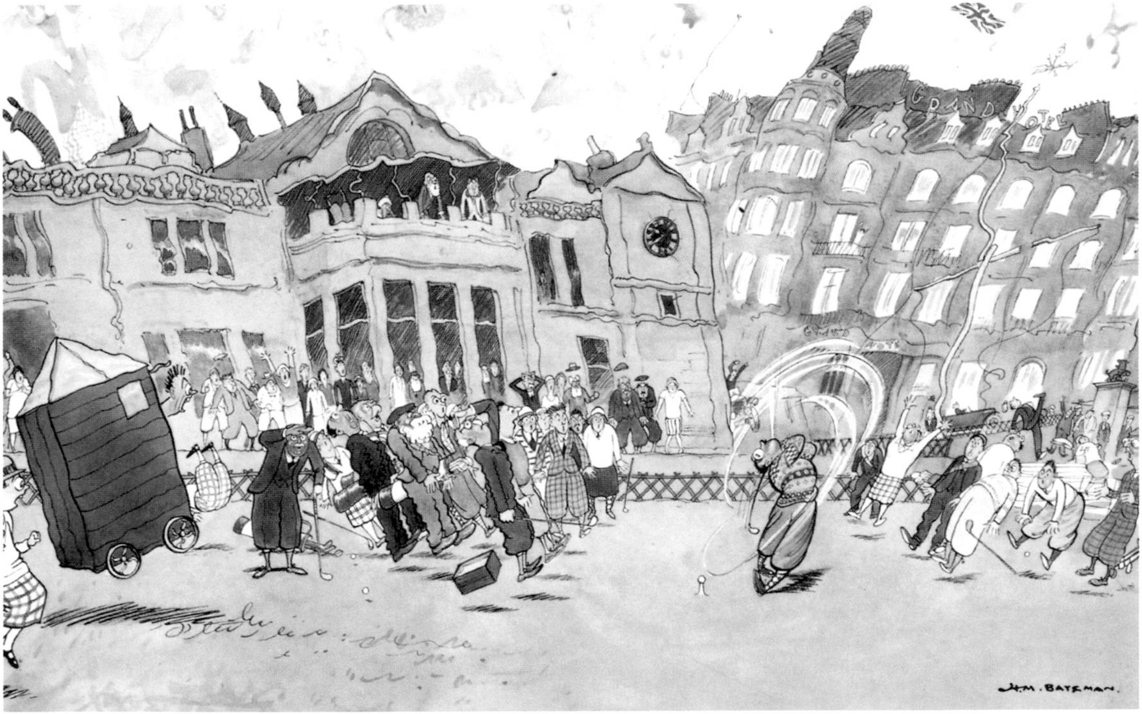
GRAND HOTEL
H.M. BATEMAN.

The Man Who Missed the Ball on the First Tee at St Andrew's

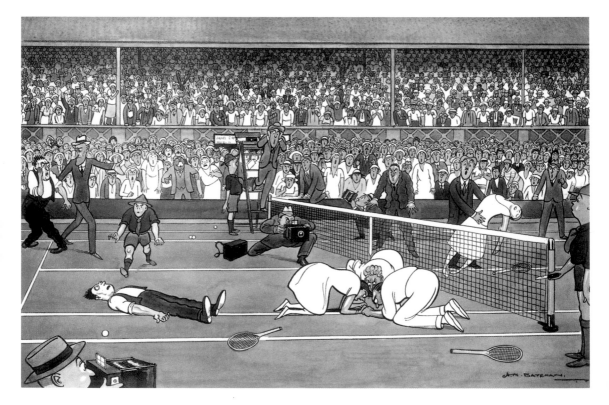

Discovery of a Dandelion on the Centre Court at Wimbledon

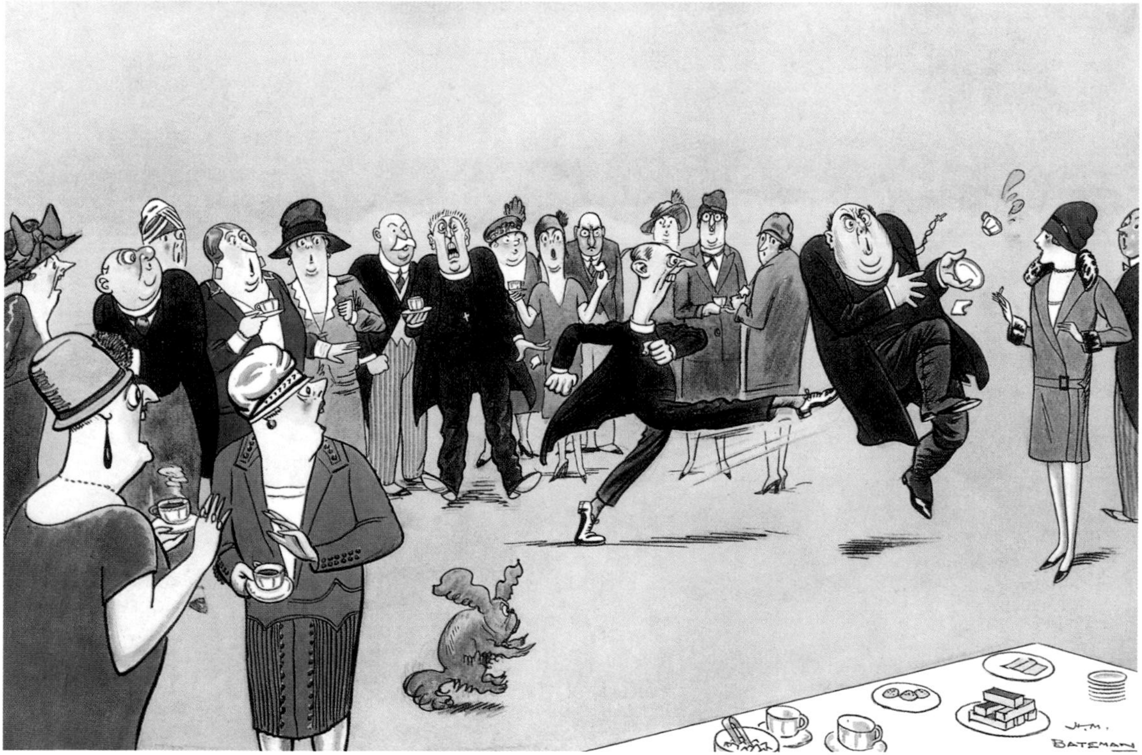
H.M. BATEMAN

The Curate Who Saw Red

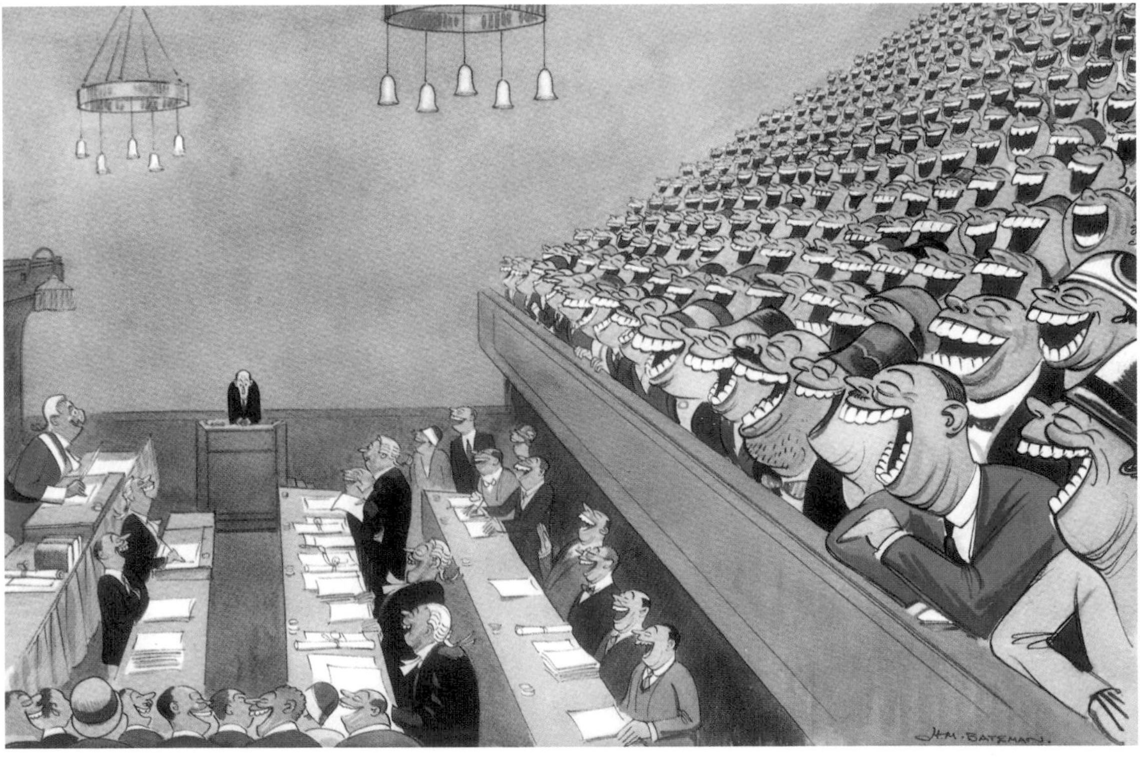
H.M. BATEMAN.

The Admission

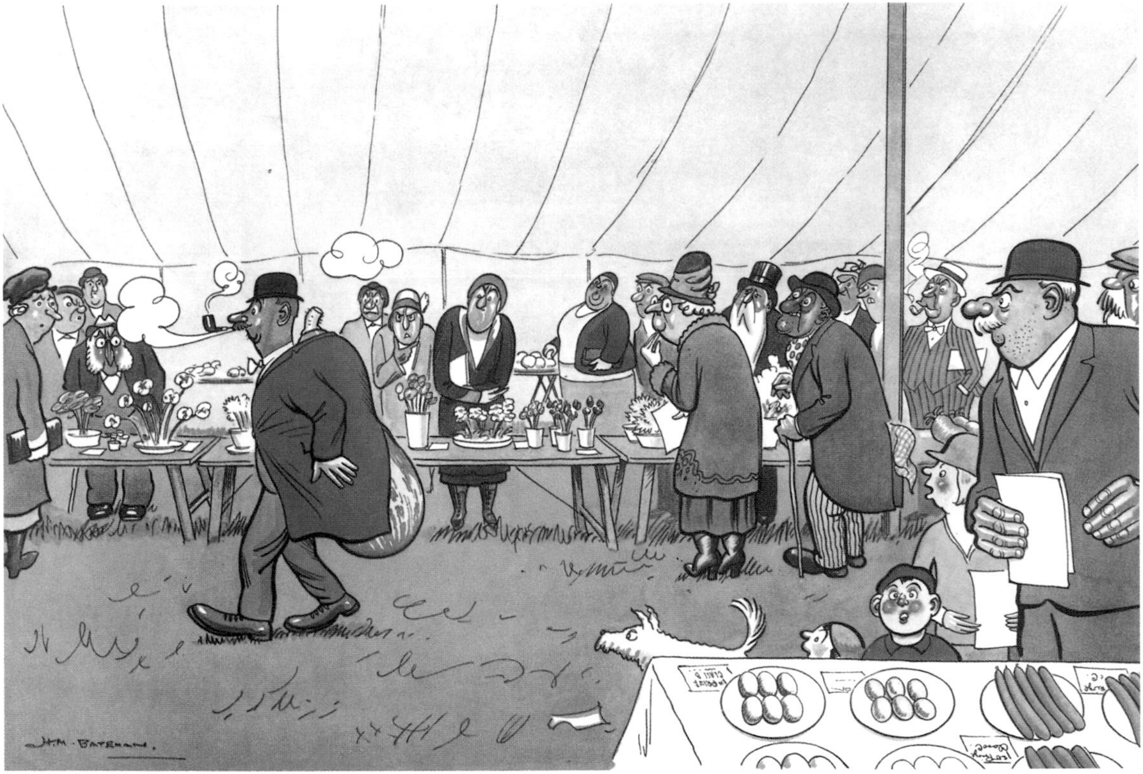
H.M. BATEMAN.

The Man Who Stole the Prize Marrow

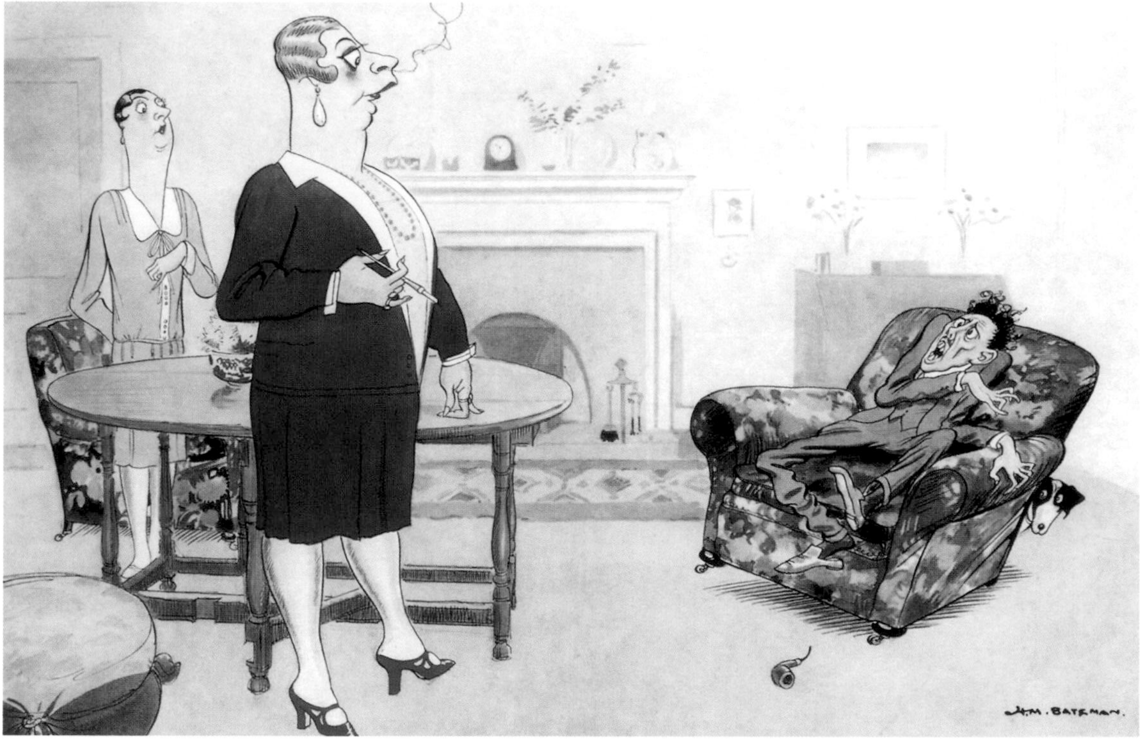
H.M. BATEMAN.

The Man Who Dared to Differ From His Mother-in-Law

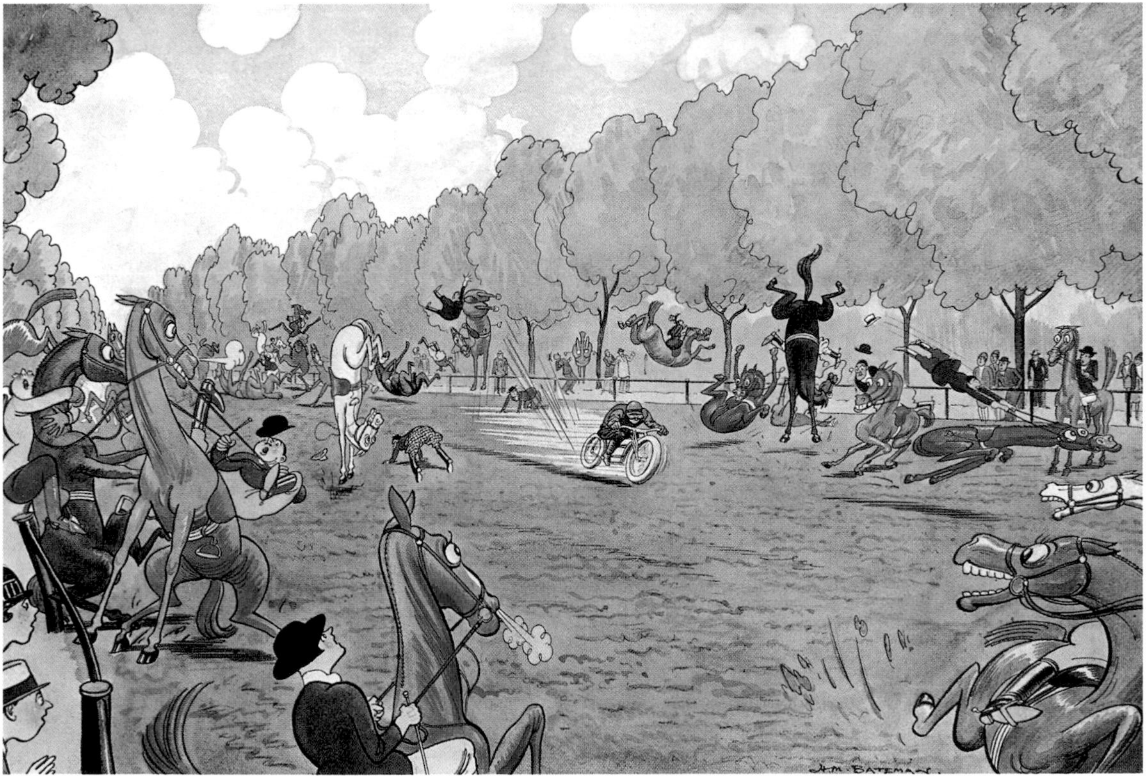
H.M. BATEMAN

The Dirt-Track Rider Who Appeared in Rotten Row

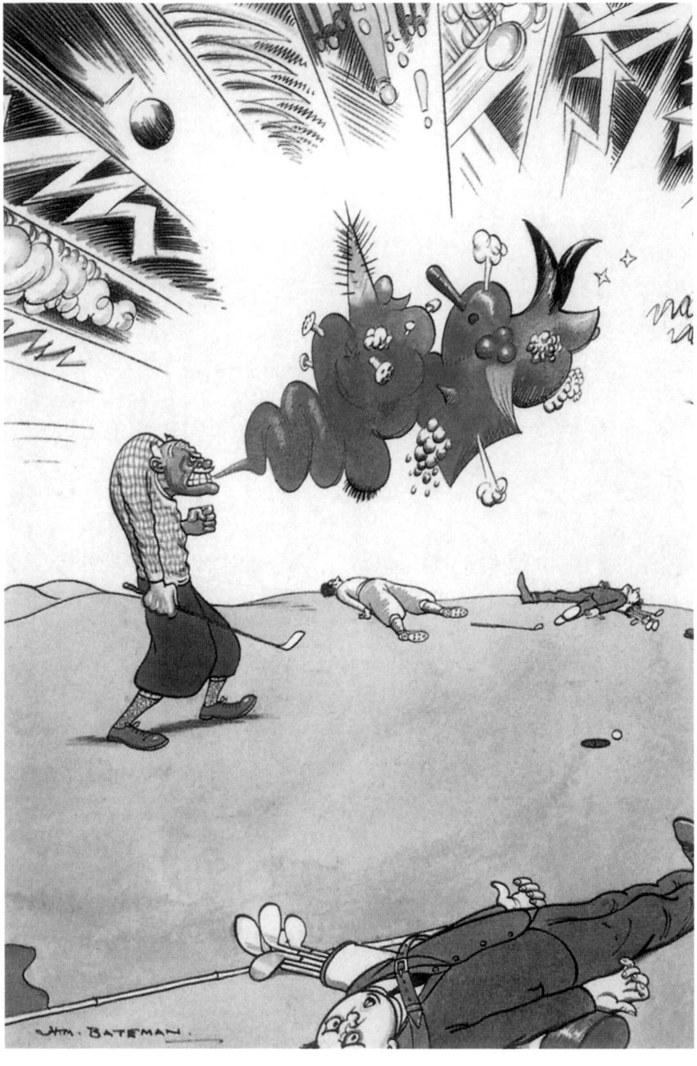
WM. BATEMAN.

The New Word in Golf

The Arts

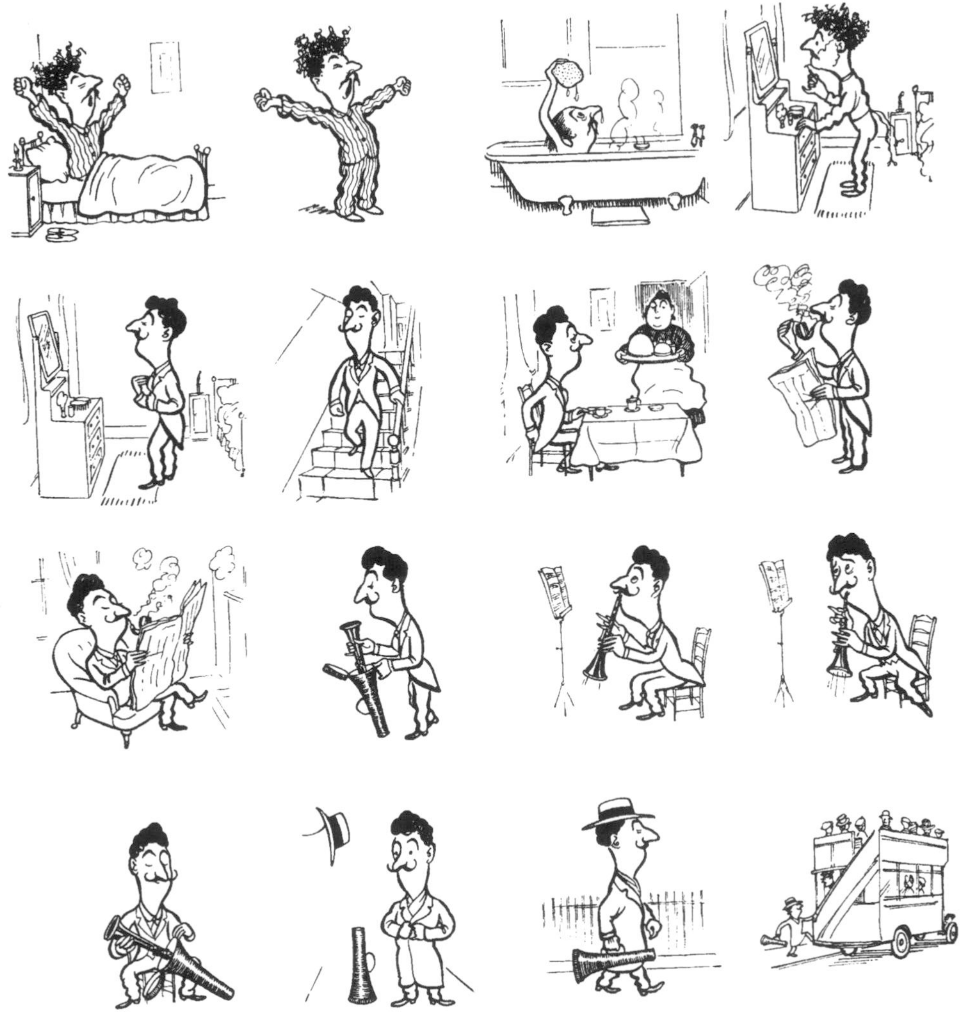

The One Note Man

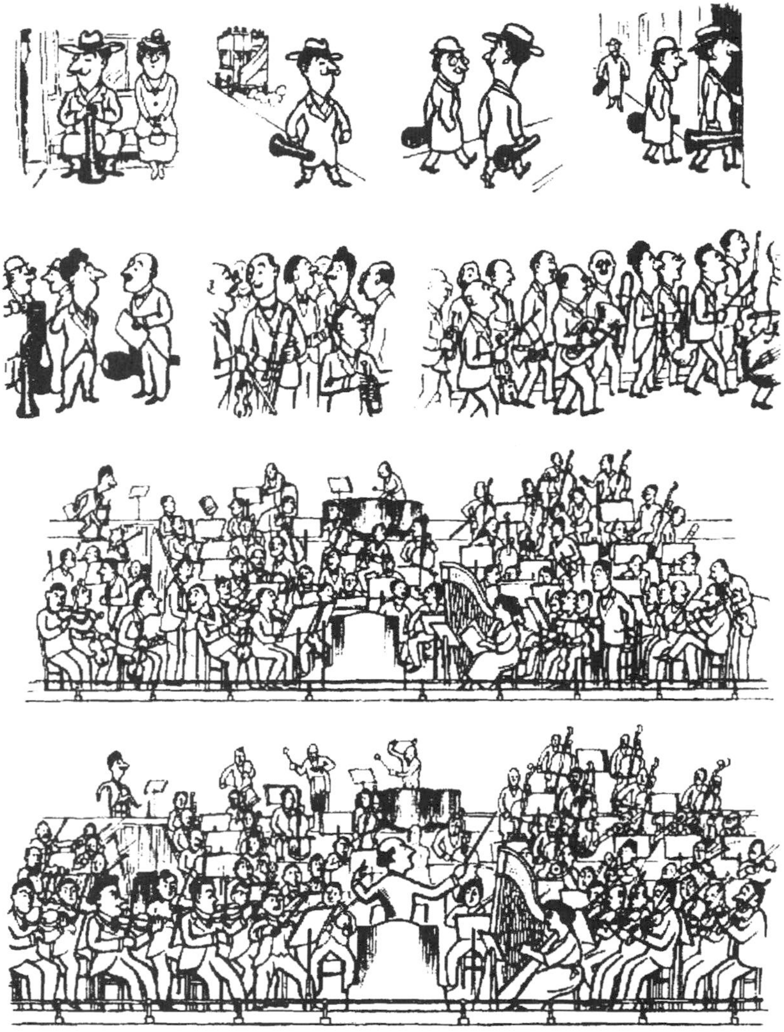

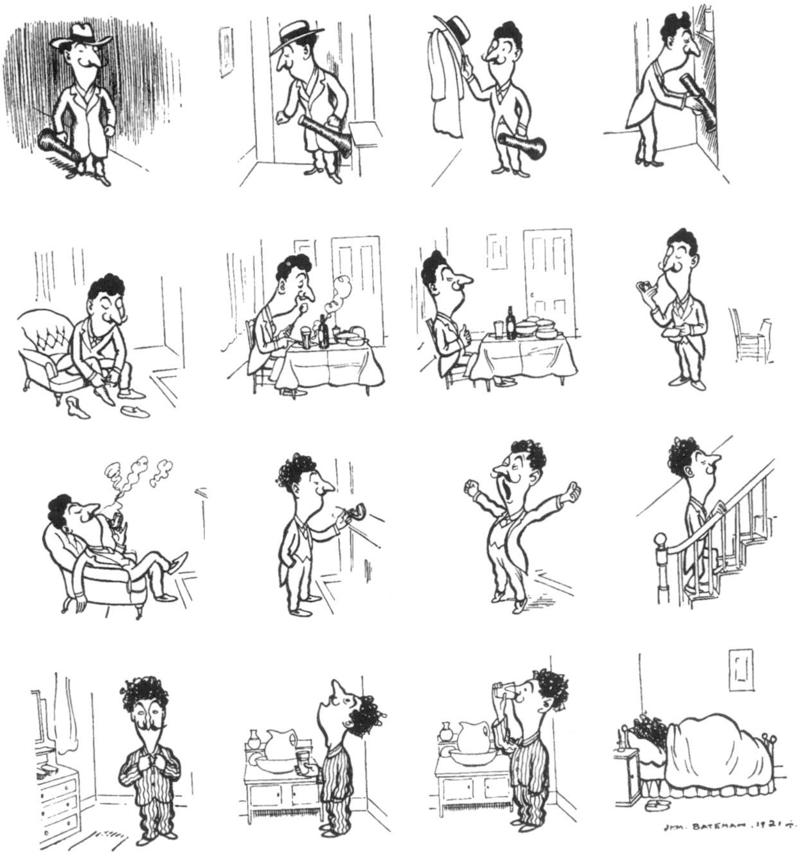
H.M. BATEMAN. 1921

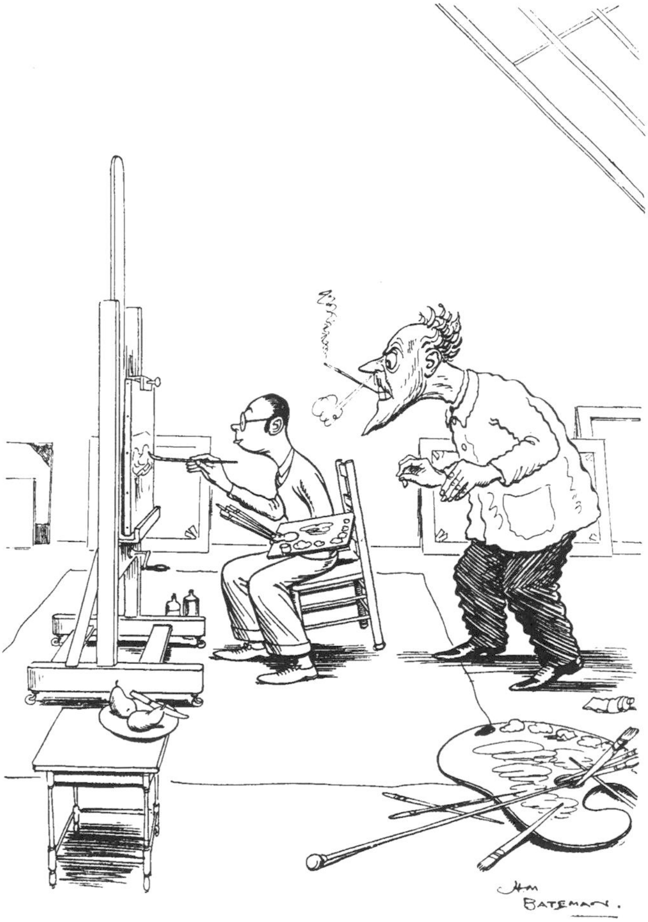
H M BATEMAN.

The Pupil Who Excelled His Master

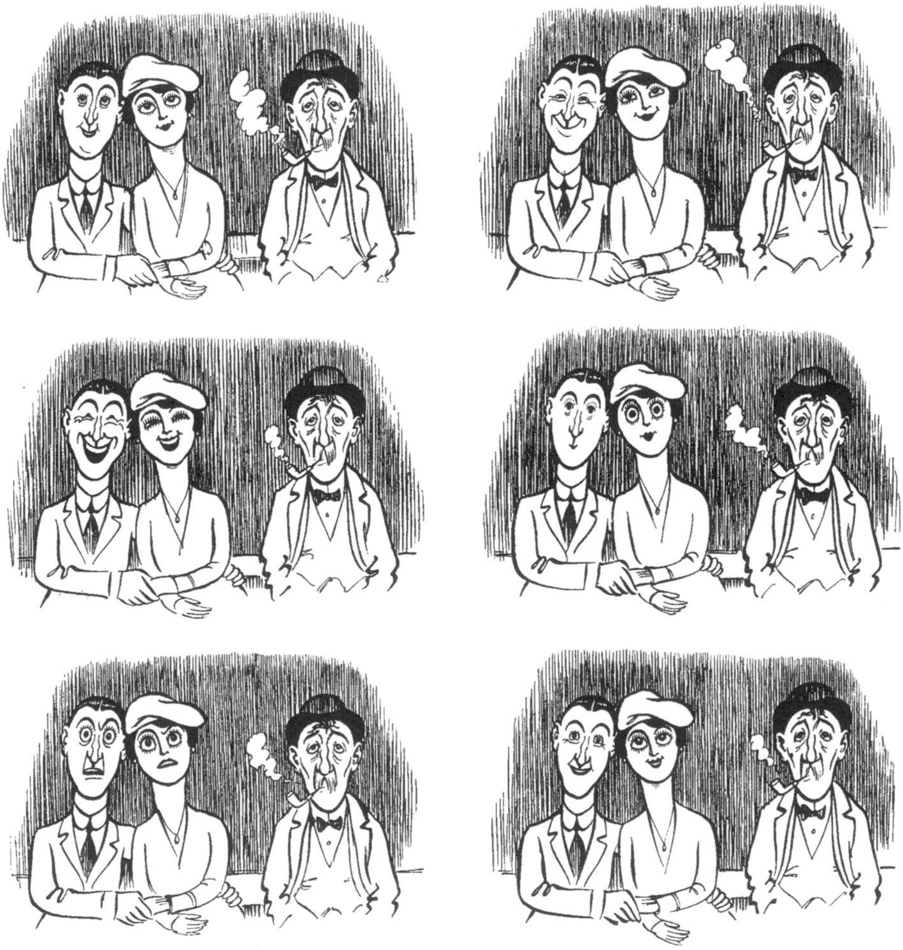

The Pictures

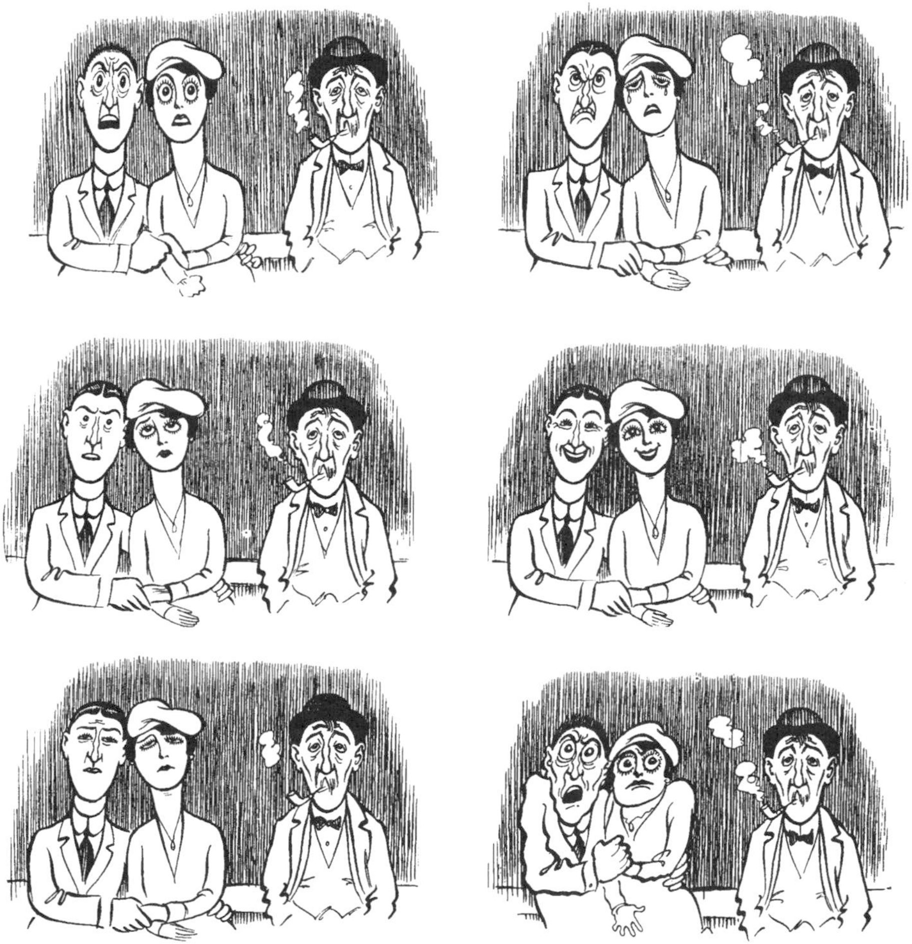

H.M.
BATEMAN

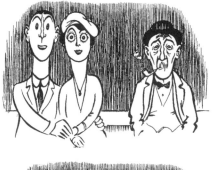

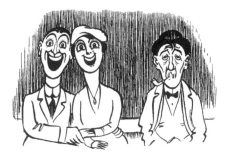

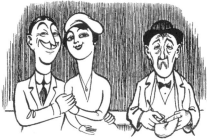

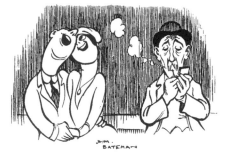

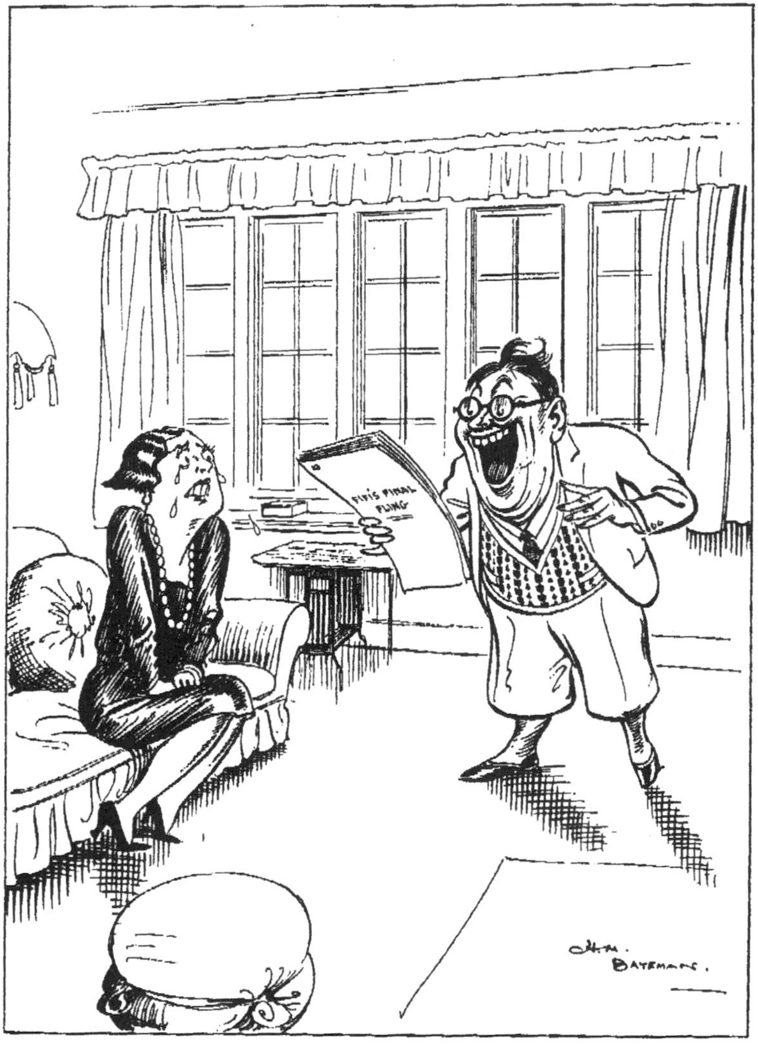
FIFI'S FINAL FLING

The Professional Humorist's Wife

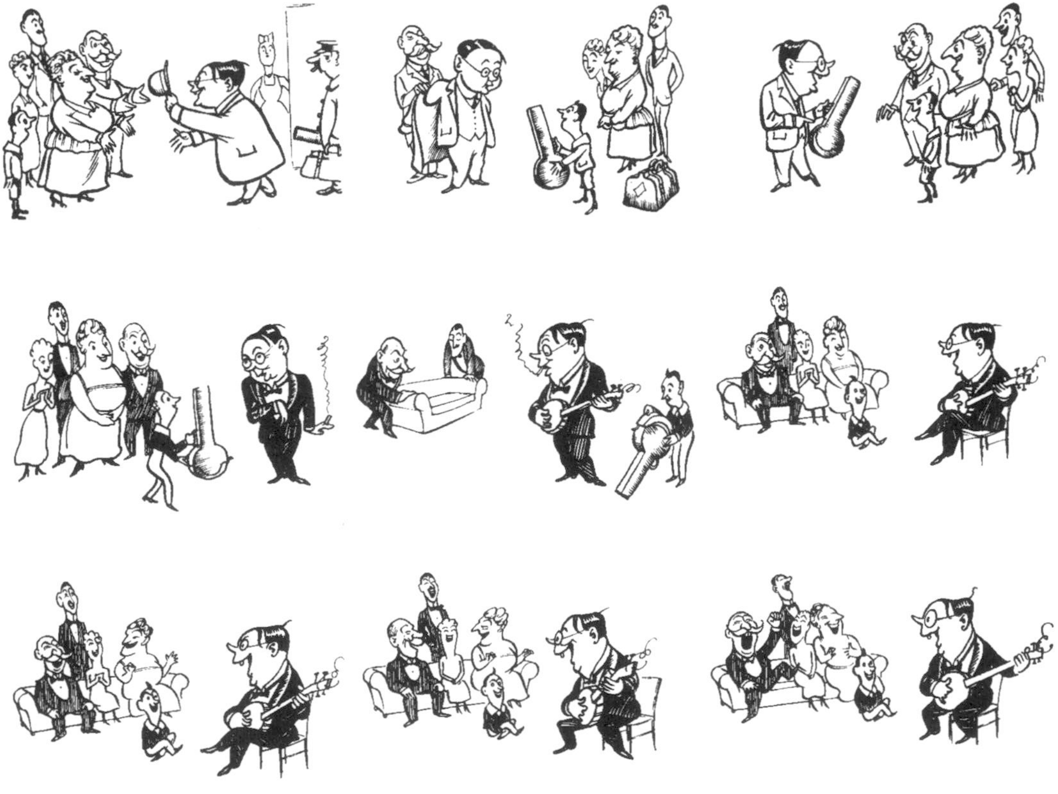

The Guest Who Bought a Banjo

H.M. BATEMAN.

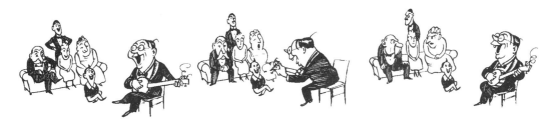

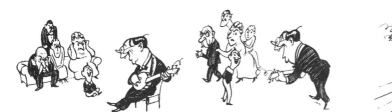

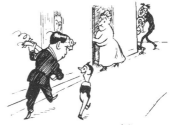

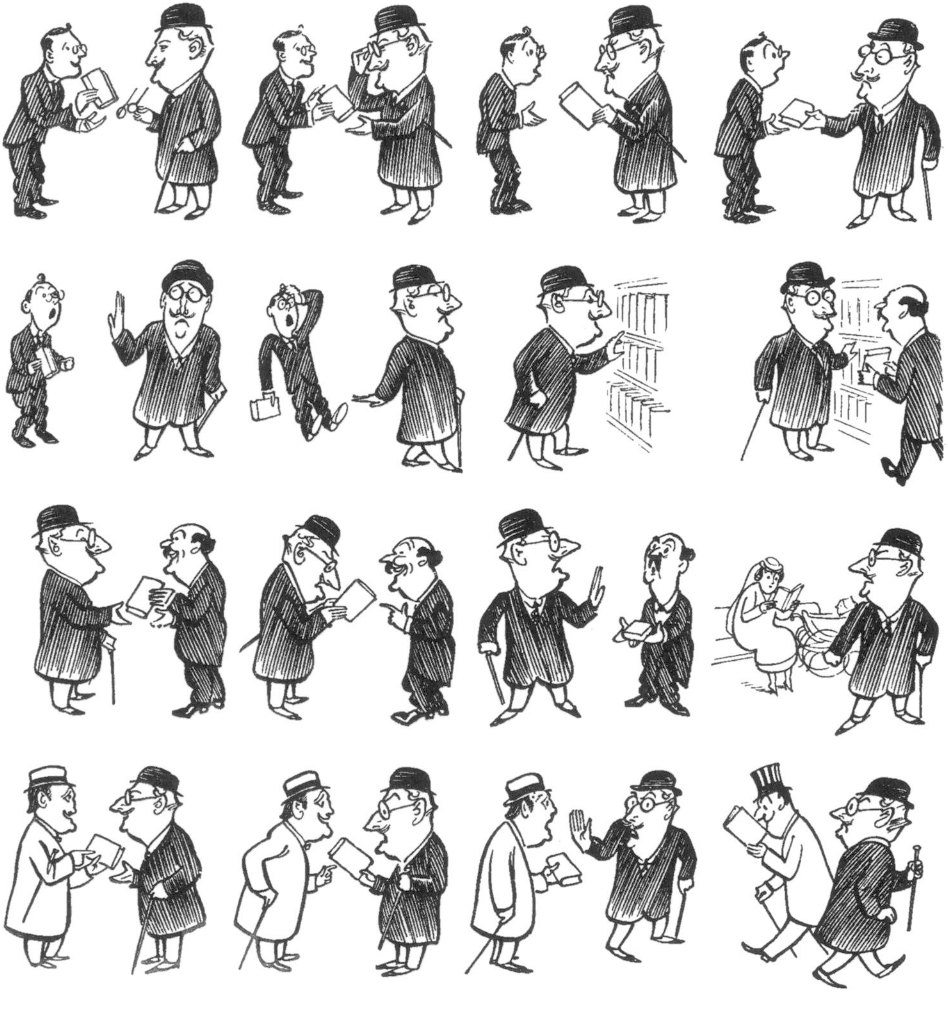

An Attempt to Evade the Bestseller

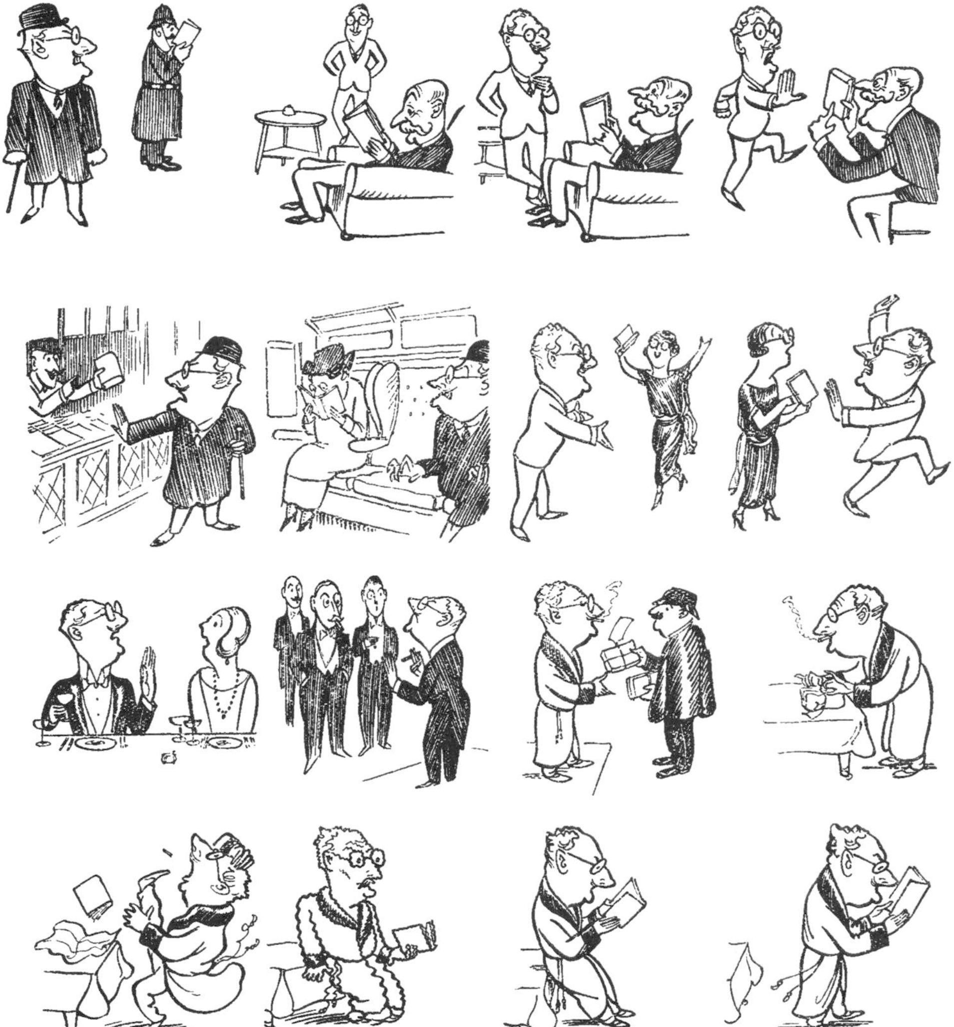

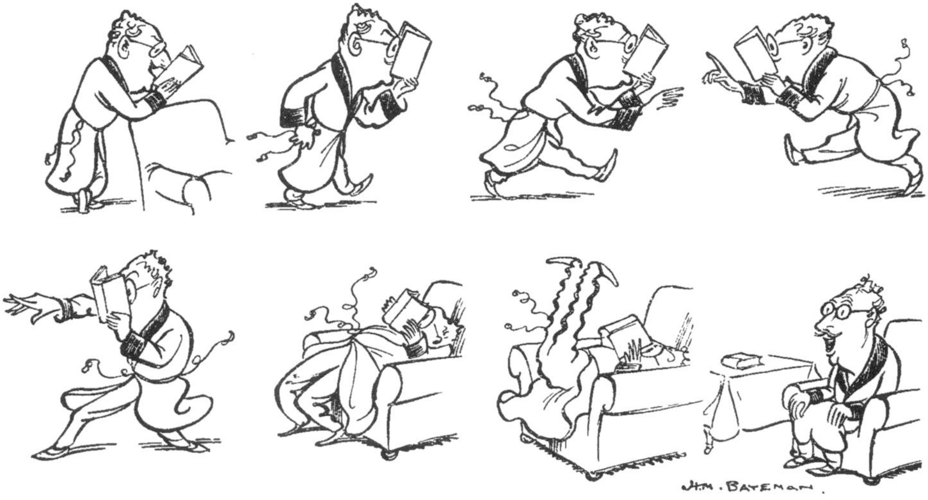
H.M. BATEMAN.

Crime and Punishment

The Boy Who Breathed on the Glass at the British Museum

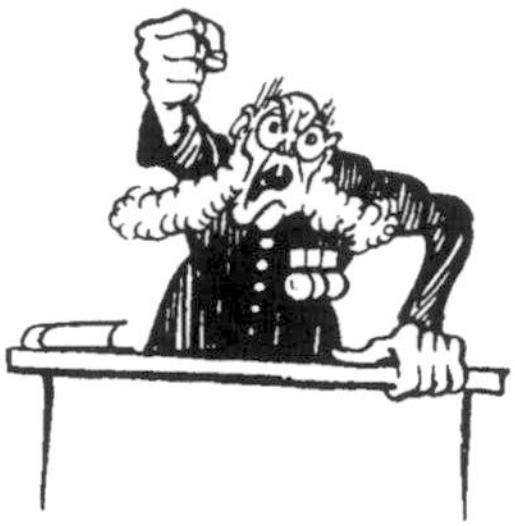
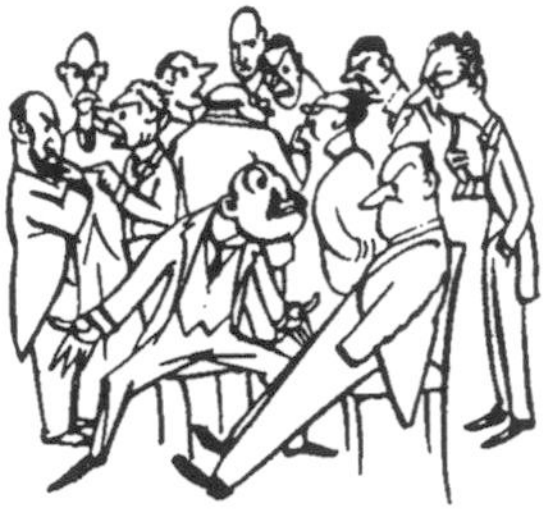
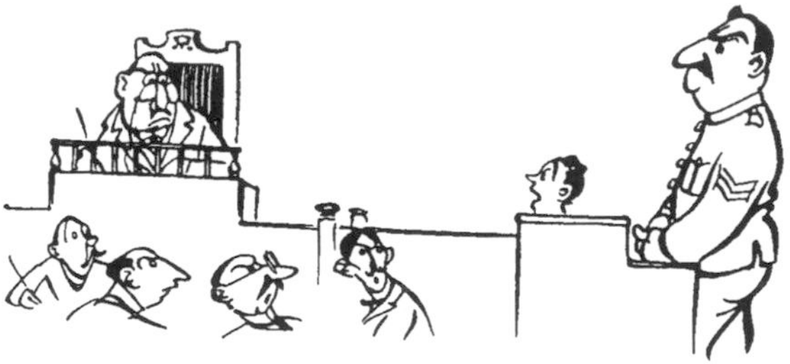
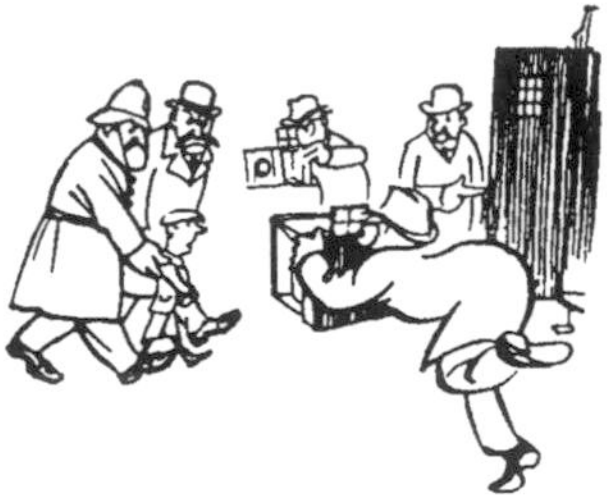
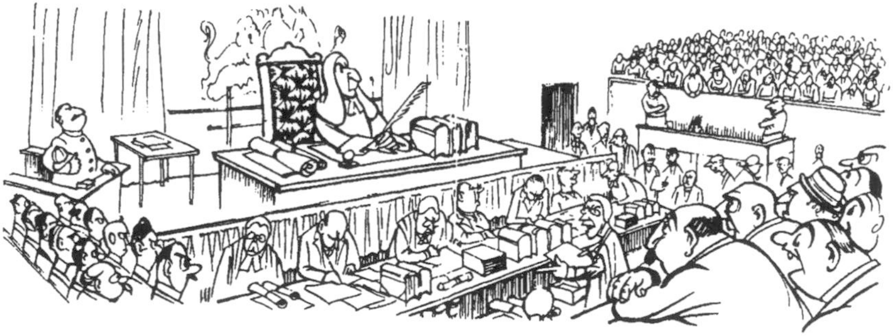

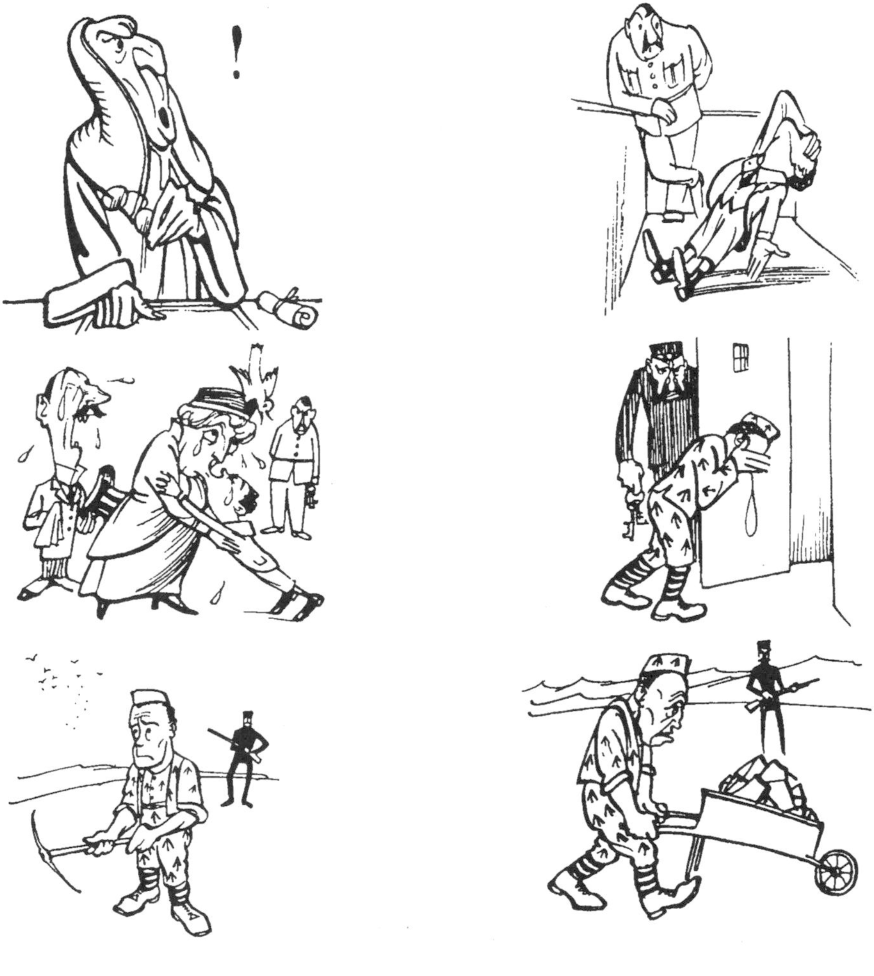

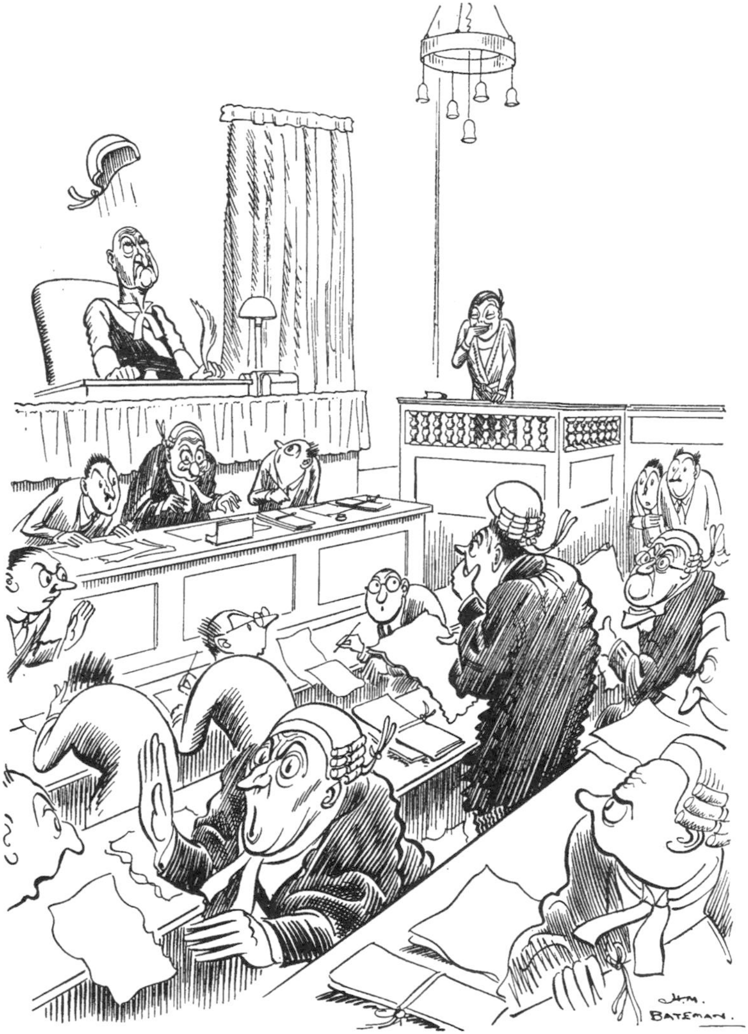
H.M.
BATEMAN.

Counsel Calls the Judge 'Mister'

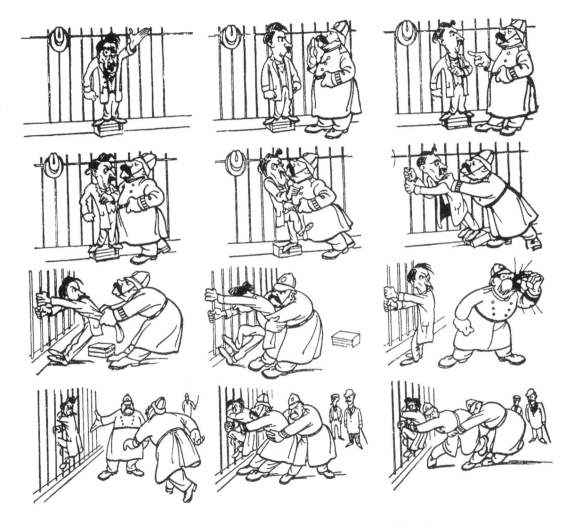

'Prisoner, When Arrested, Clung to the Railings'

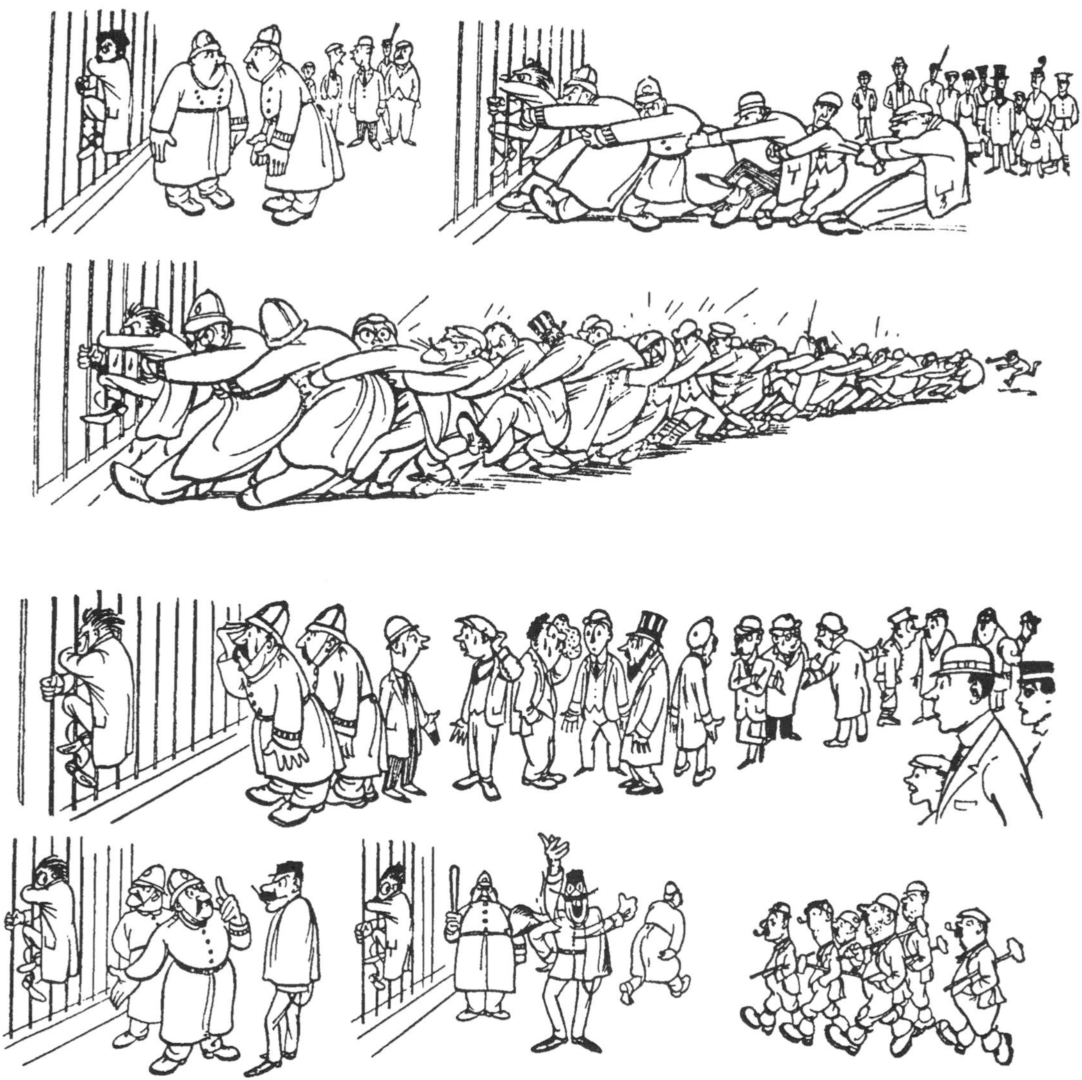

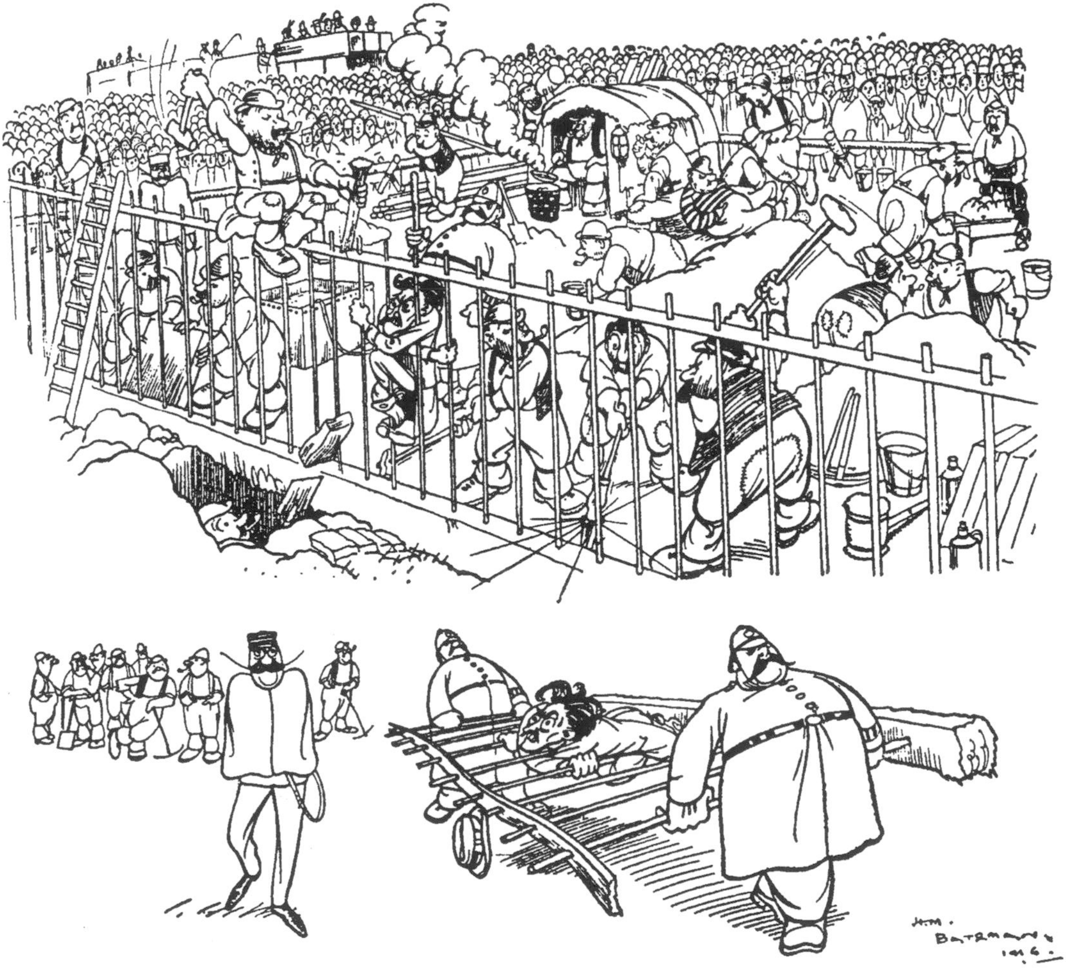
H.M. BATEMAN 1916

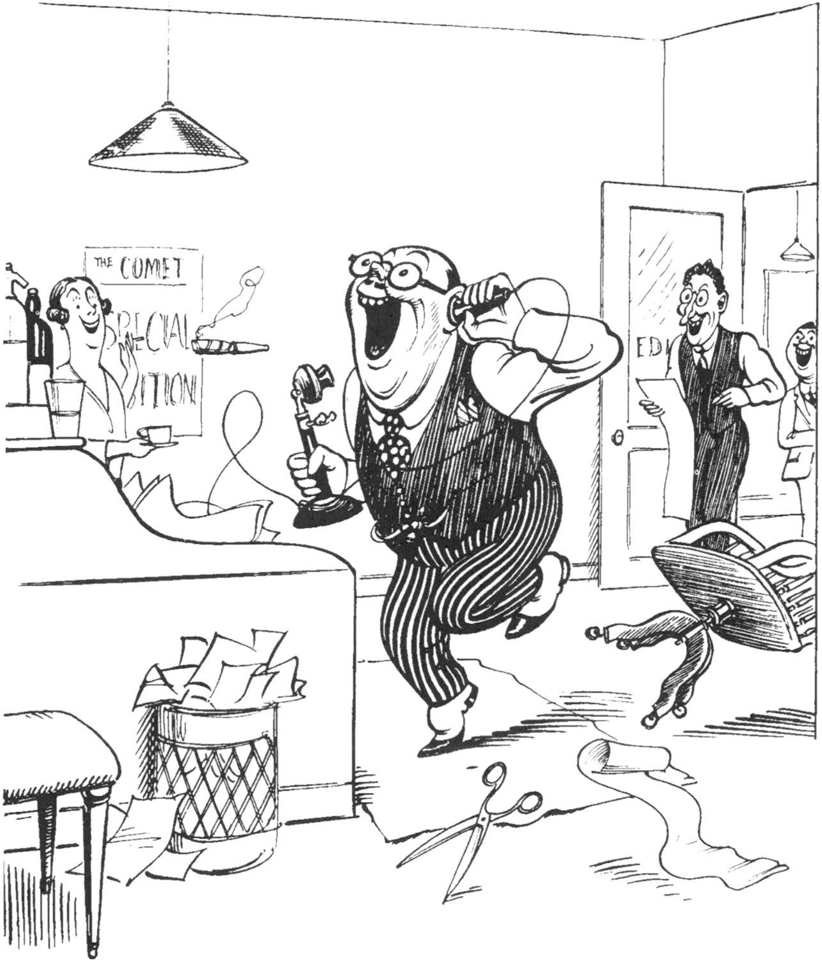
THE COMET

The Editor of a Yellow Press Newspaper Receiving News of a Horrible Murder Committed in Circumstances of the Most Revolting Atrocity

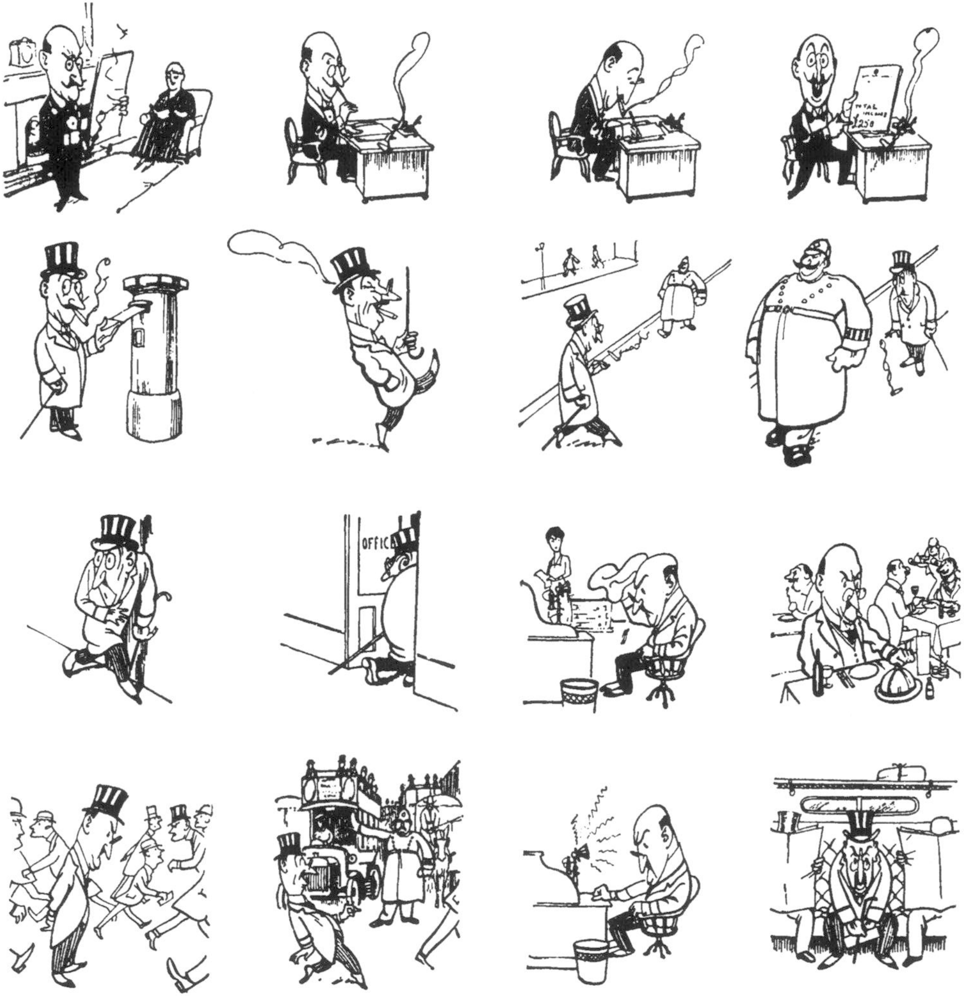
OFFIC

The False Income Tax Return – and Its Rectification

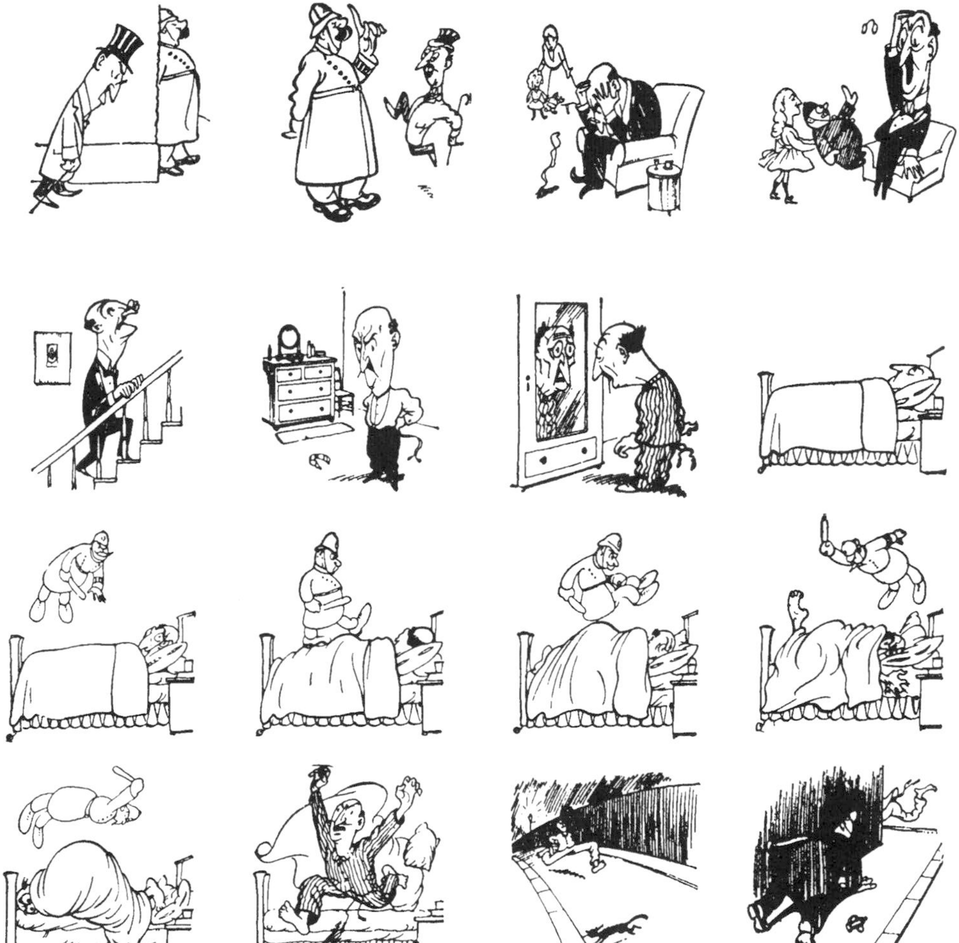

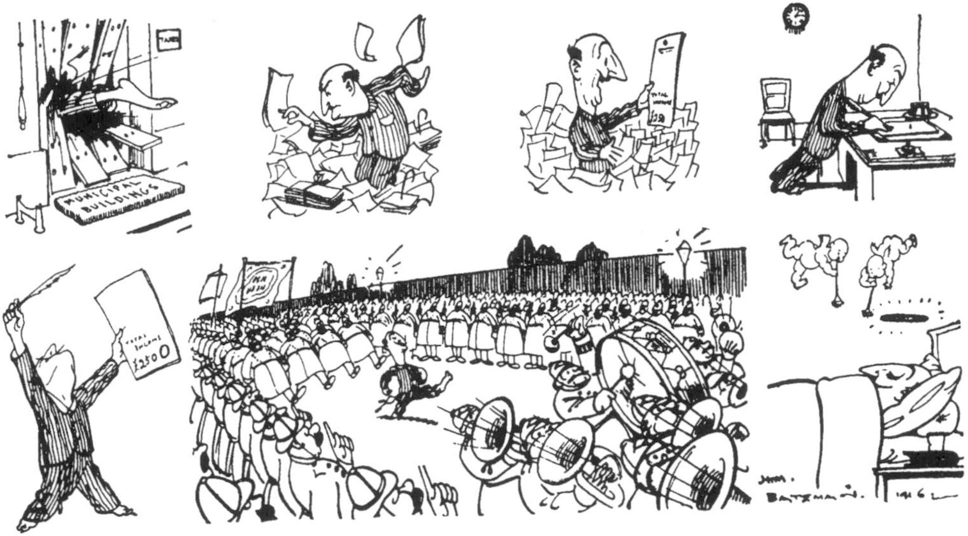
MUNICIPAL BUILDINGS
TOTAL INCOME £2500
H.M. BATEMAN. 1946

Food and Drink

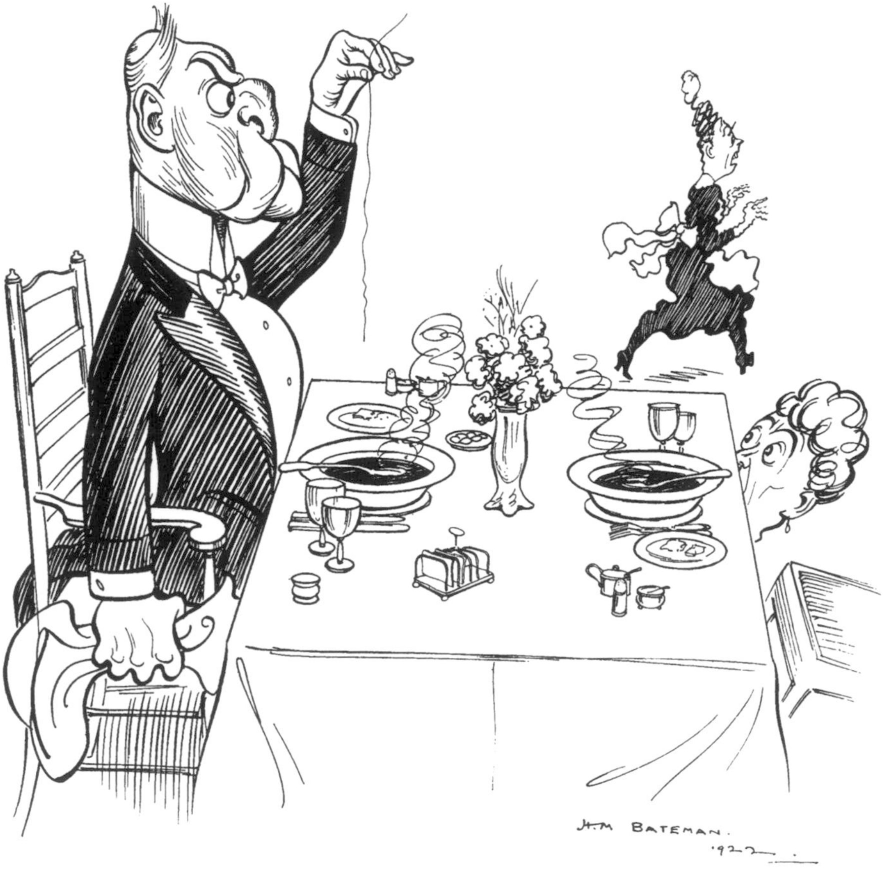
H.M BATEMAN.

A Hair in the Soup

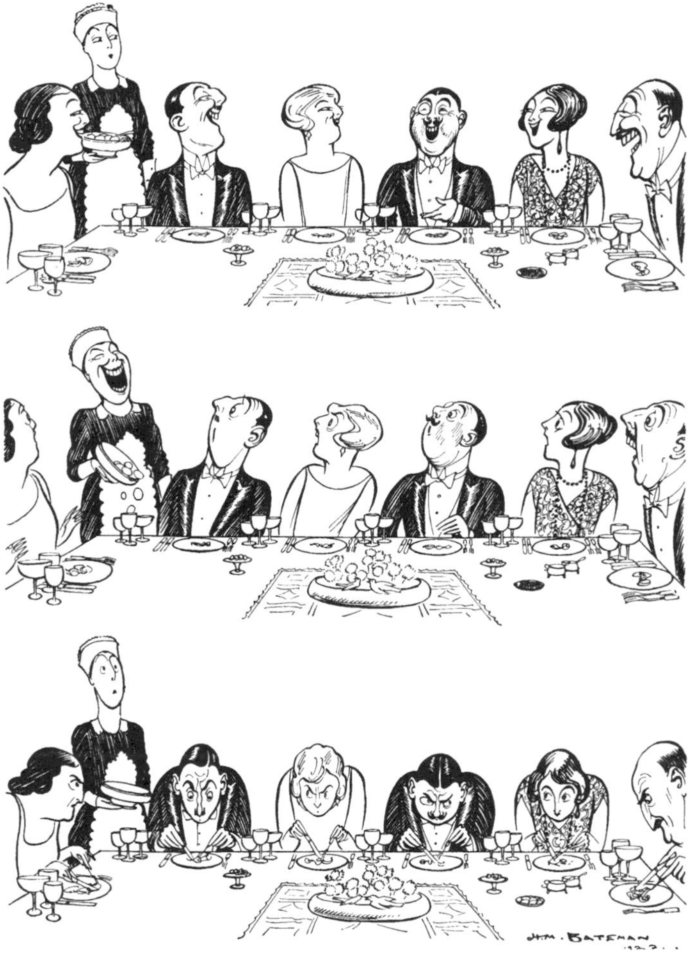
H.M. BATEMAN

The Maid Who Was But Human

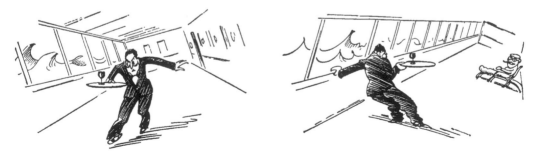

Trials of a Steward

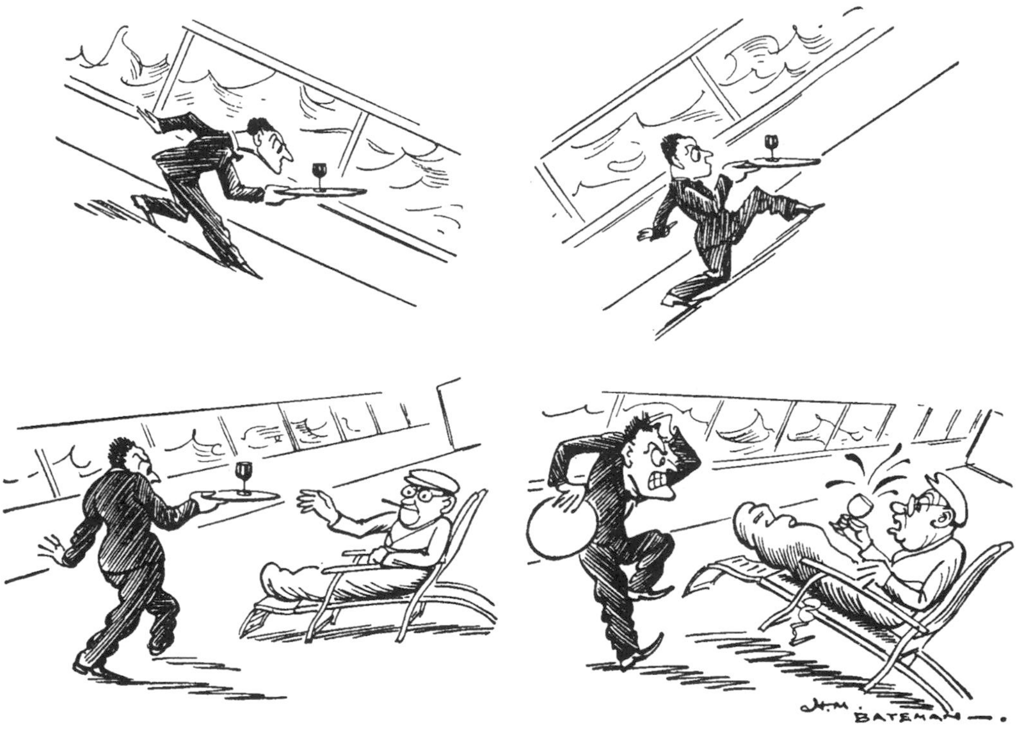
H. M. BATEMAN

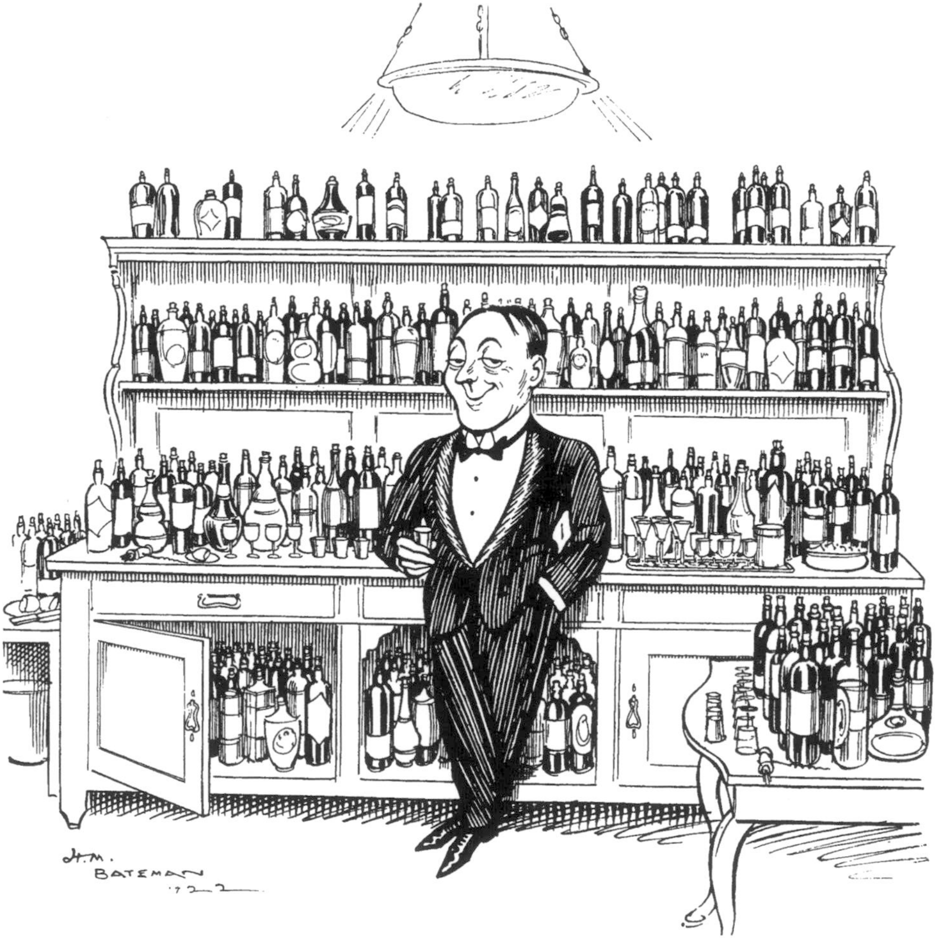
H.M.
BATEMAN

The Cocktail King

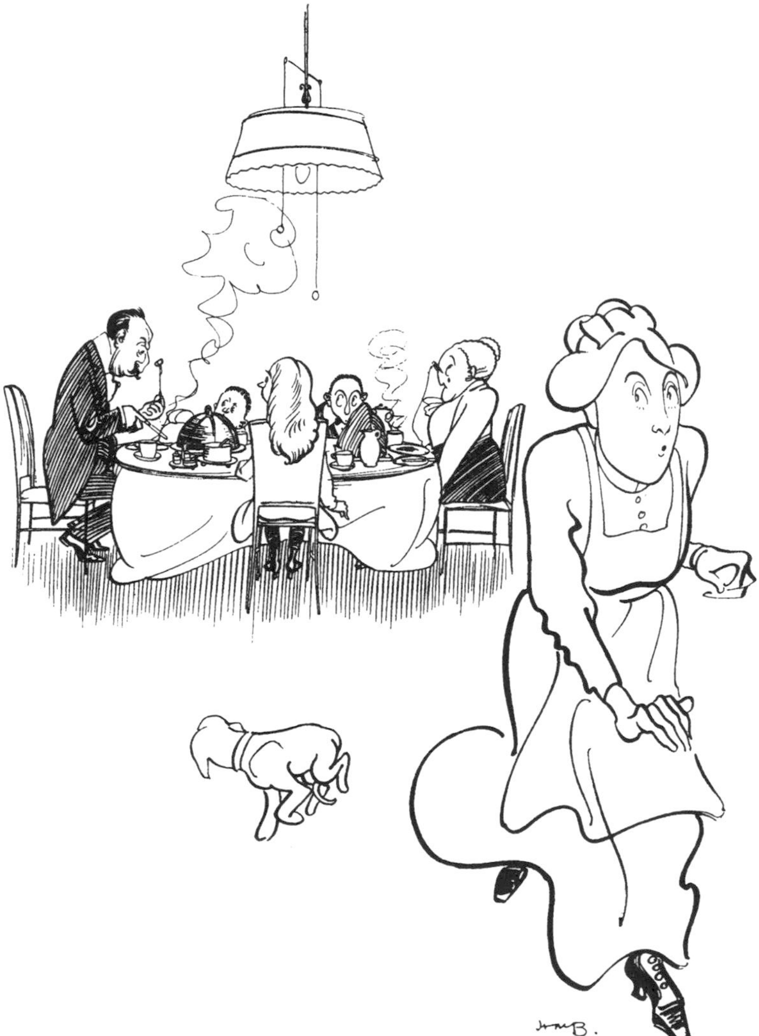
H.M.B.

Breakfast – the Difficult Meal

The Plum That Took the Wrong Turning

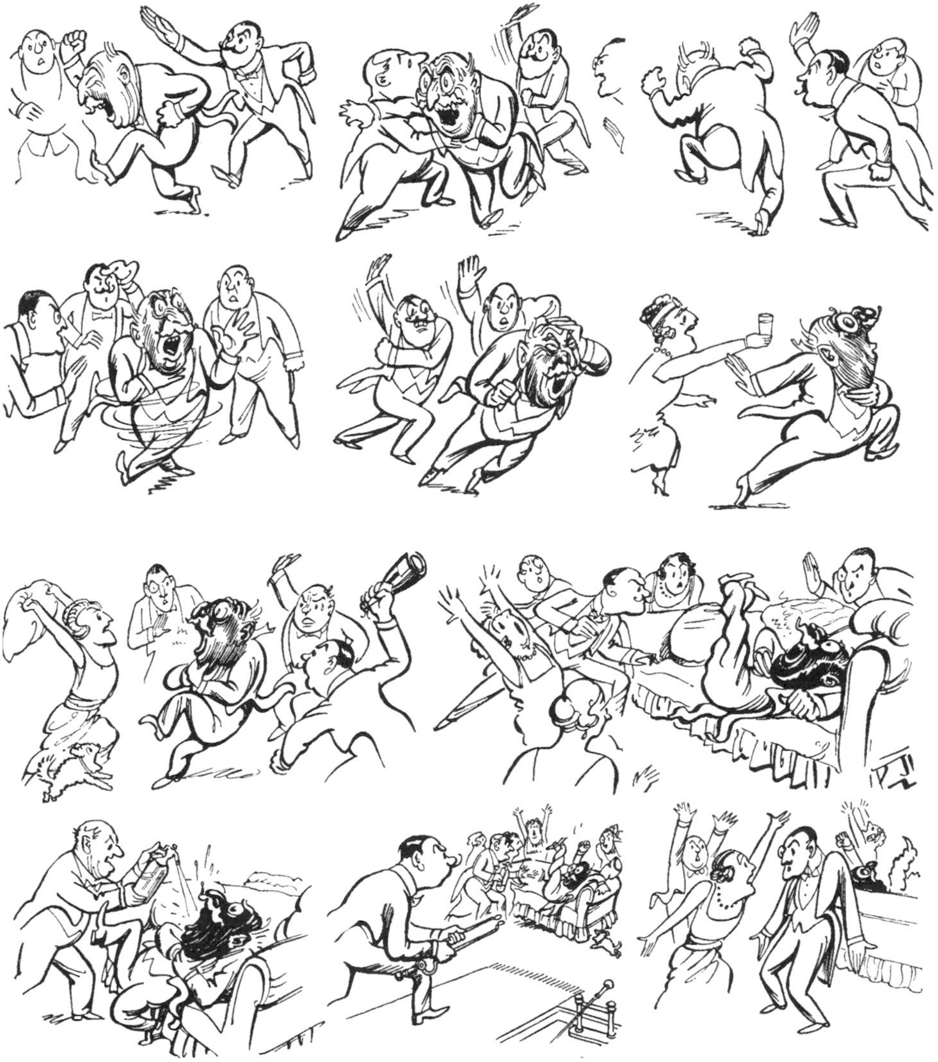

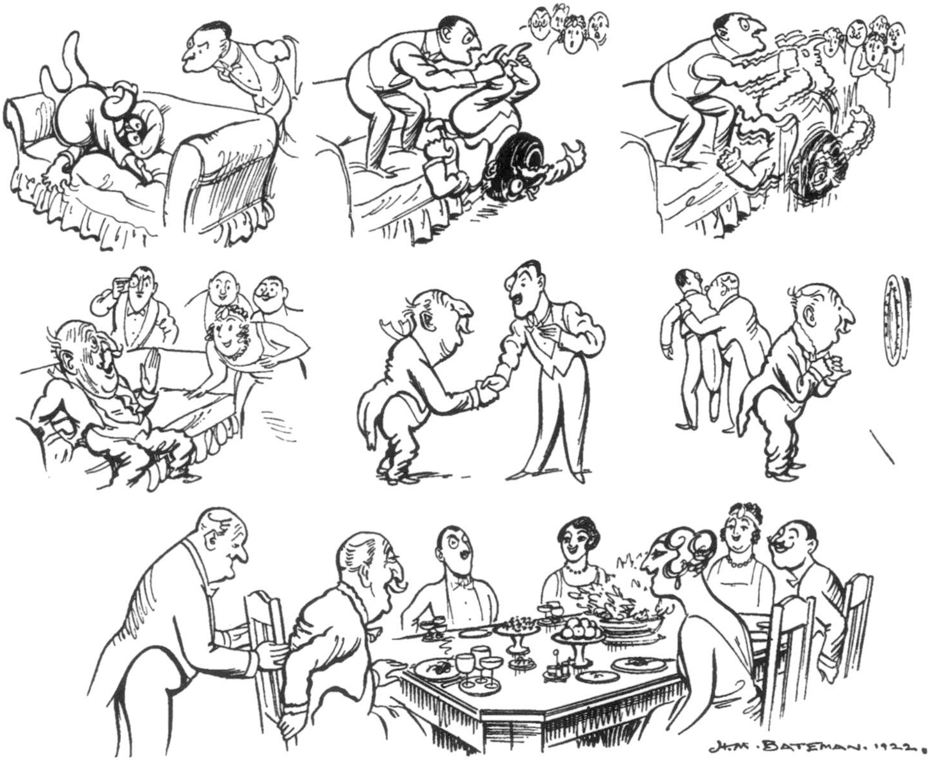
H.M. BATEMAN. 1922.

A Miscellany

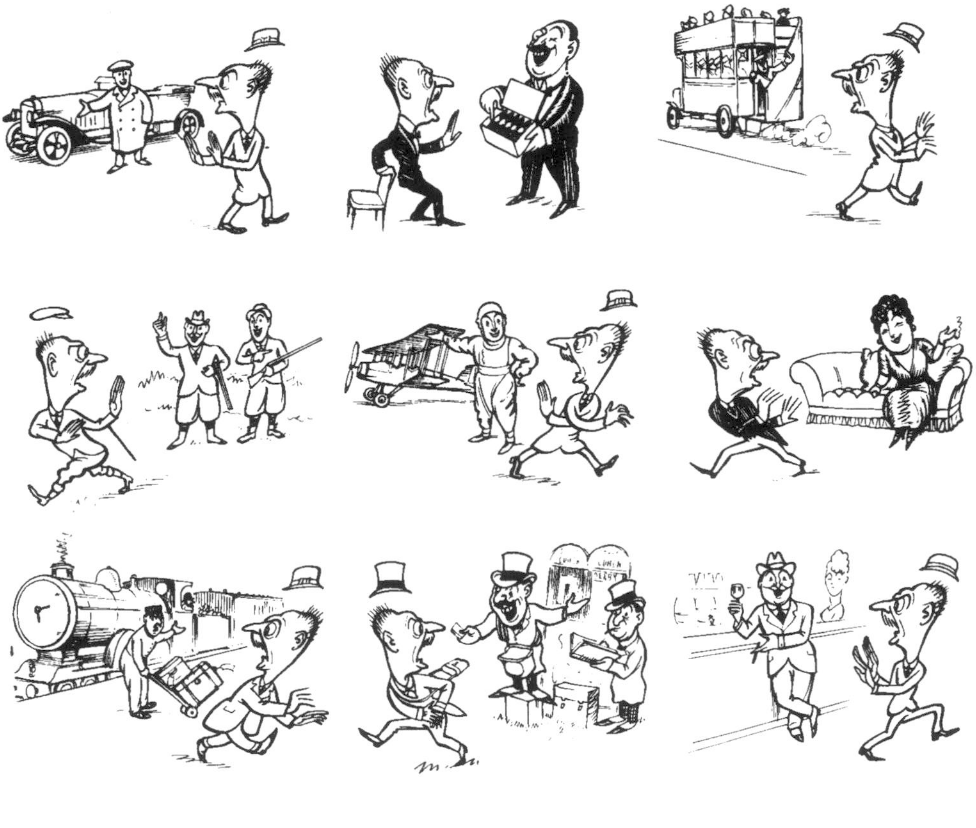

The Cautious Life

H.M. BATEMAN-21

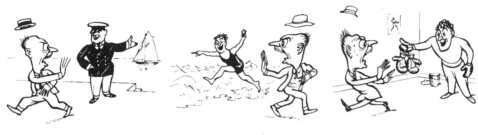

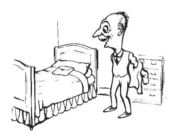

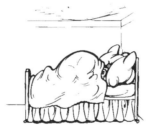

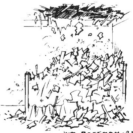

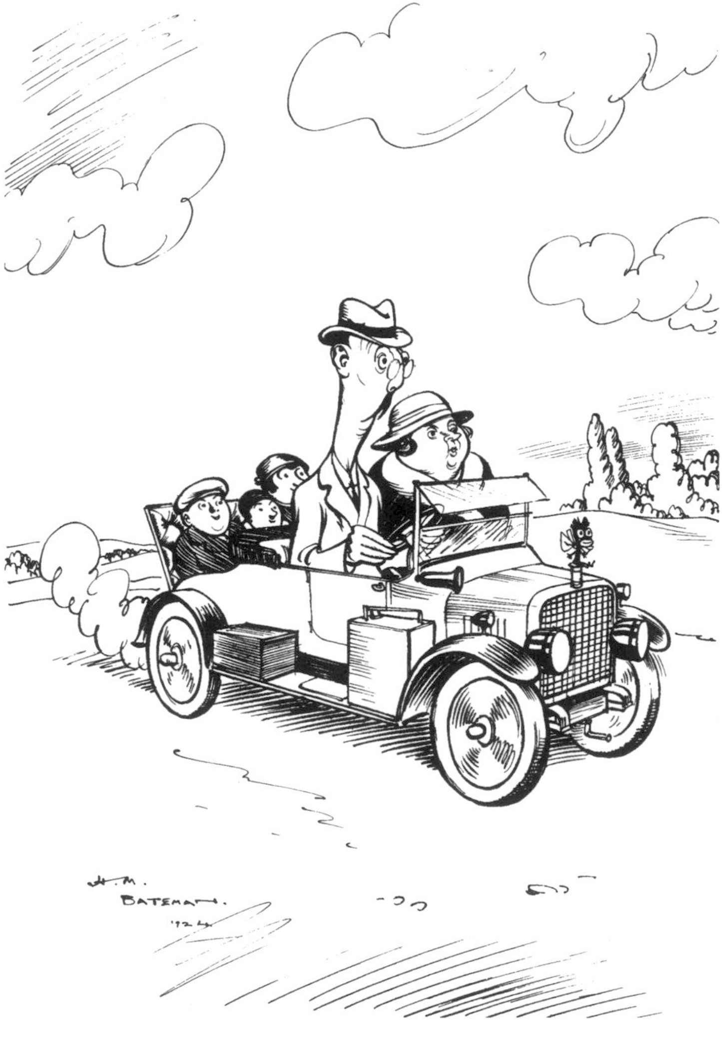
H. M. BATEMAN.

The Man Who Has Never Exceeded the Speed Limit

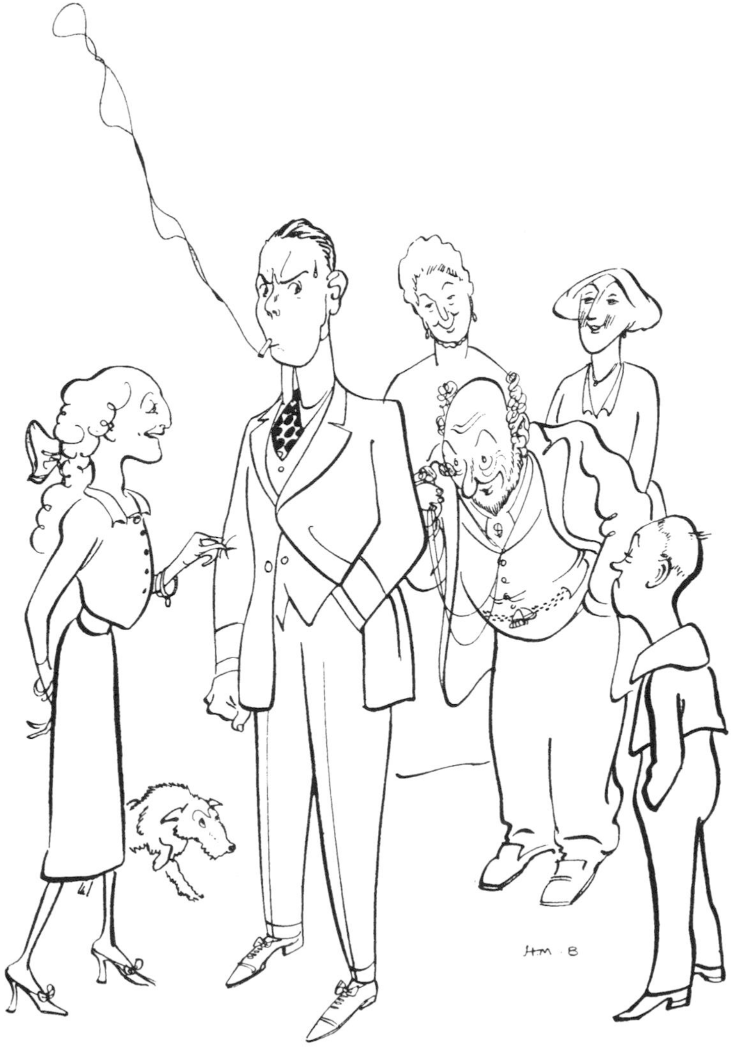

The New Suit

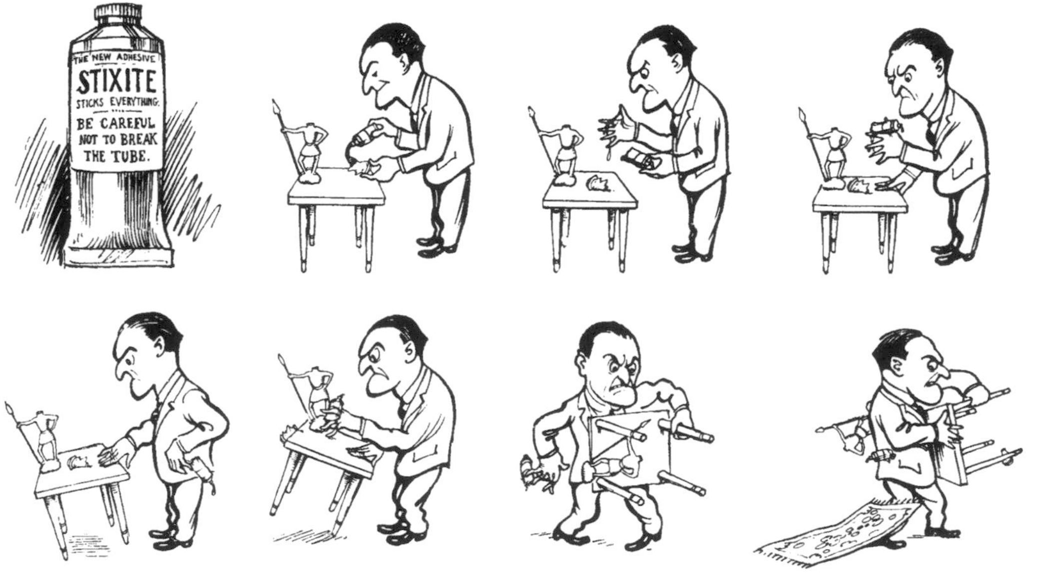
THE NEW ADHESIVE
STIXITE
STICKS EVERYTHING.
BE CAREFUL
NOT TO BREAK
THE TUBE.

The Man Who Broke the Tube

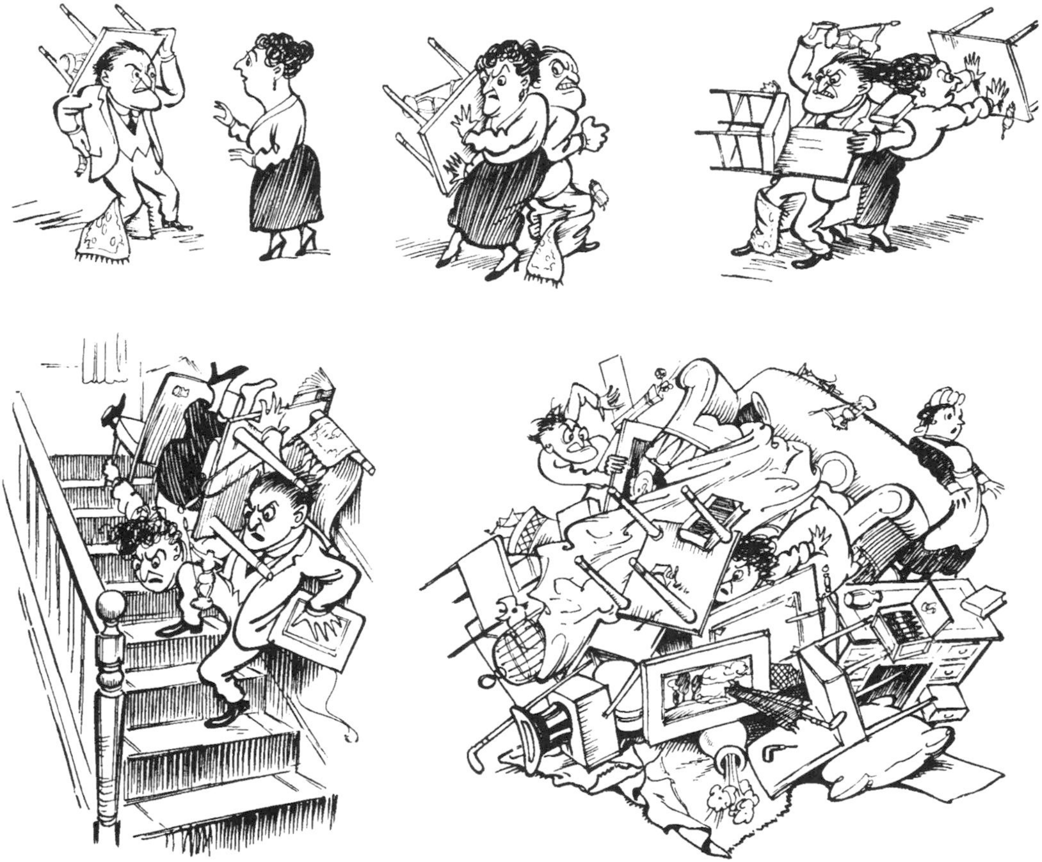

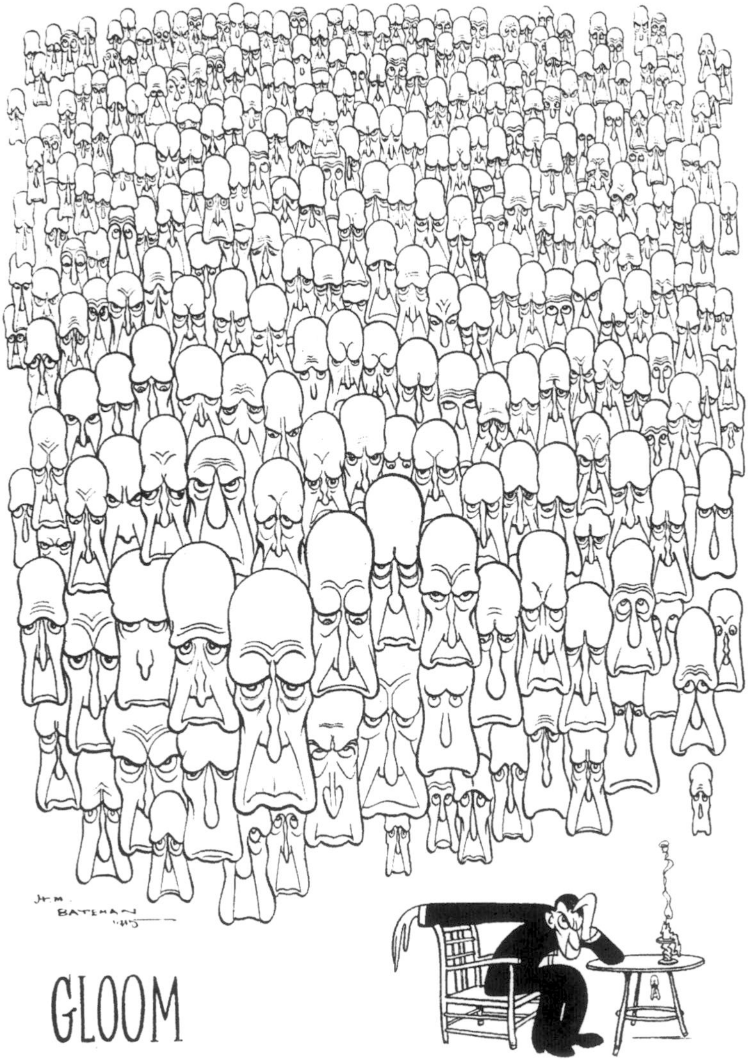
H.M. BATEMAN

GLOOM

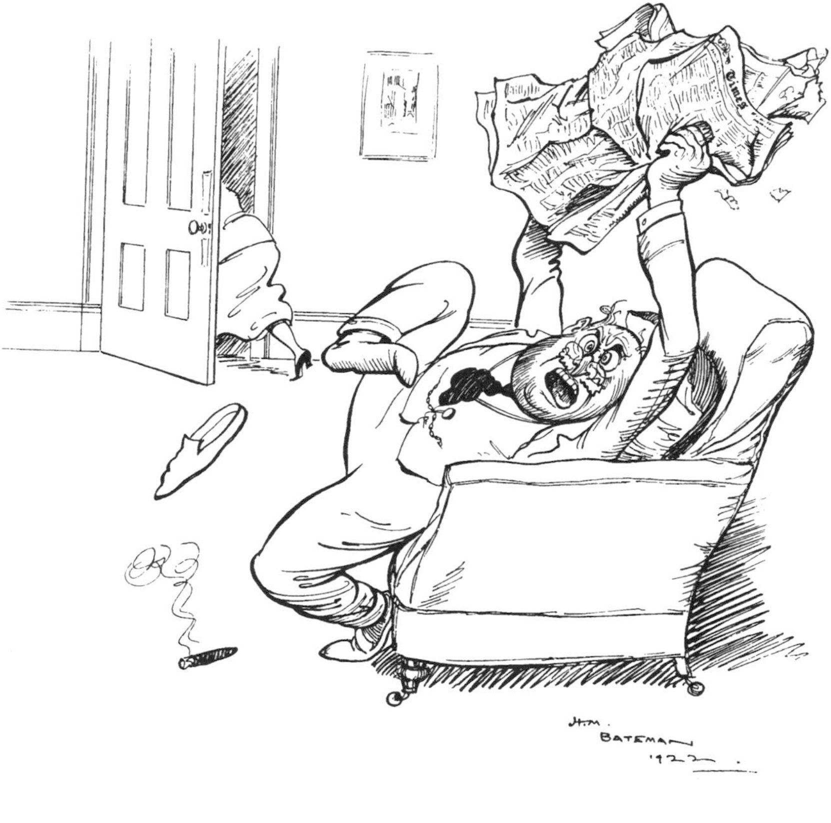
Times
H.M. BATEMAN 1922.

A Quiet Half-Hour With *The Times*

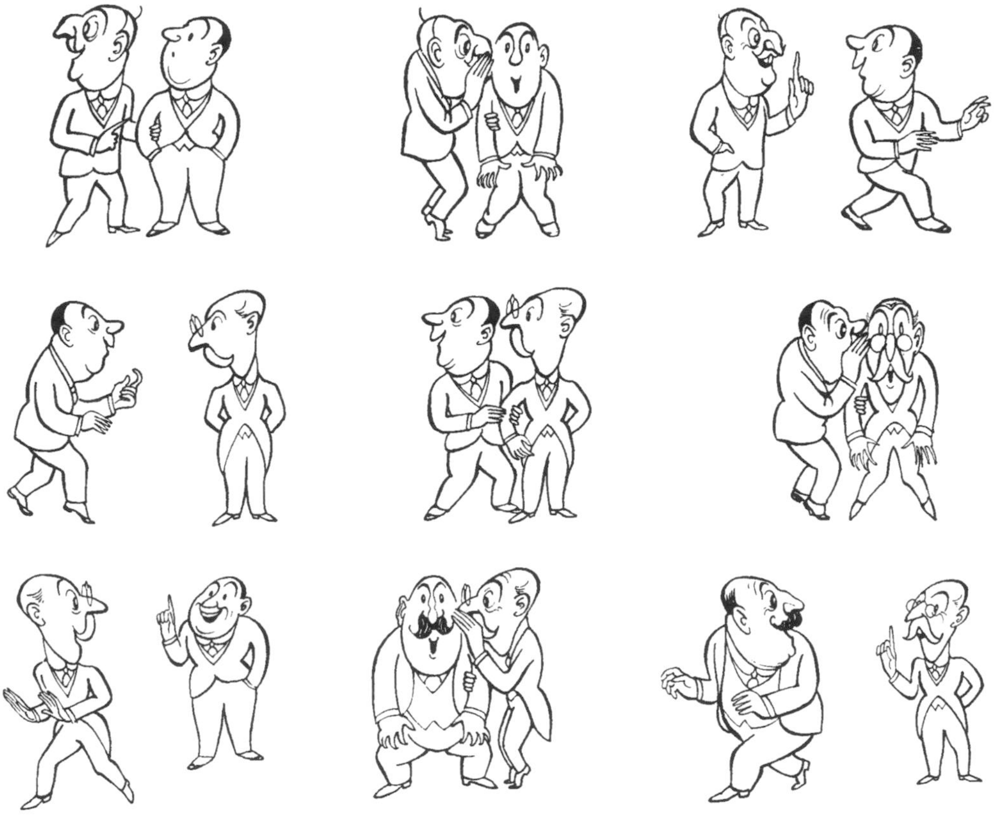

The Secret

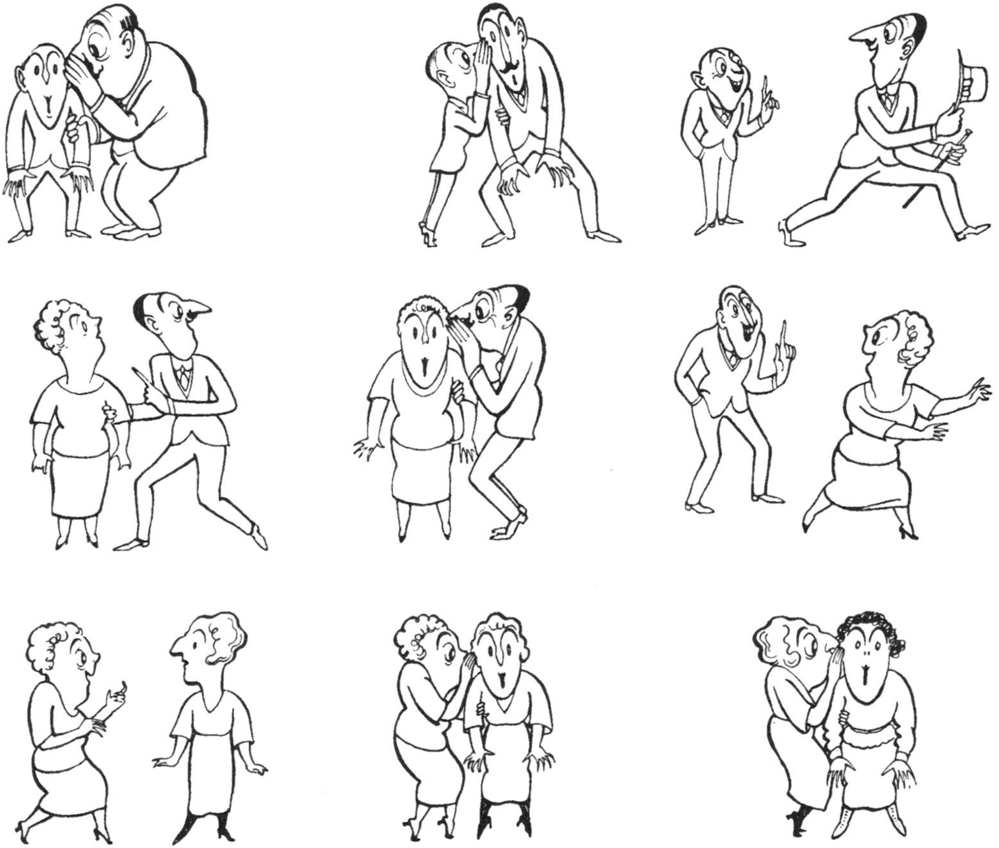

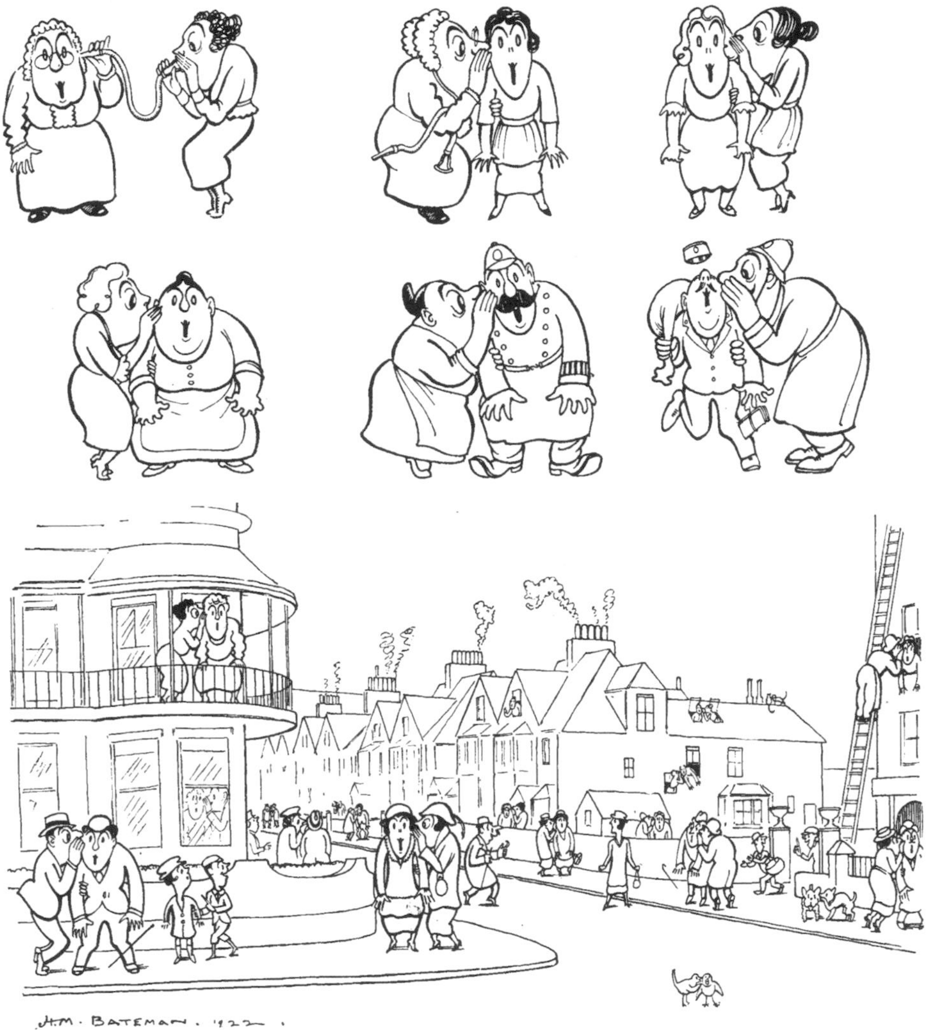
H.M. BATEMAN. 1922.

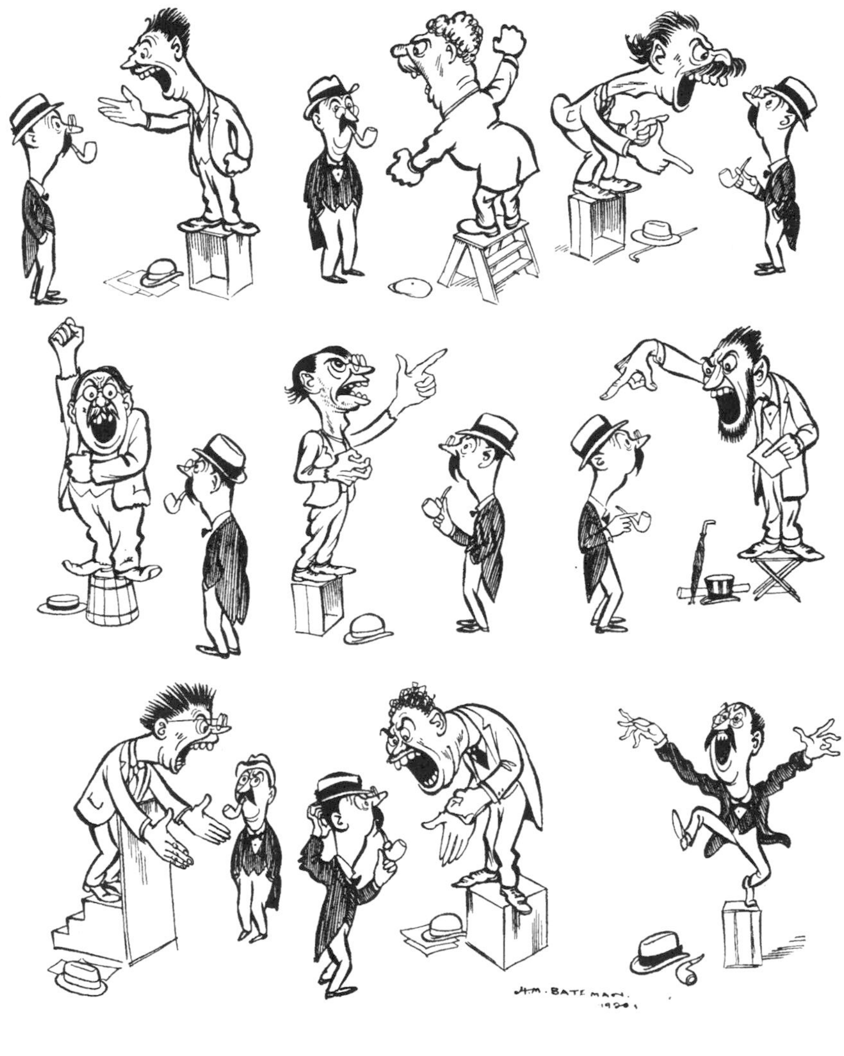
H.M. BATEMAN.
1920.

The Making of a Reformer
Showing the Infectious Influence of Oratory

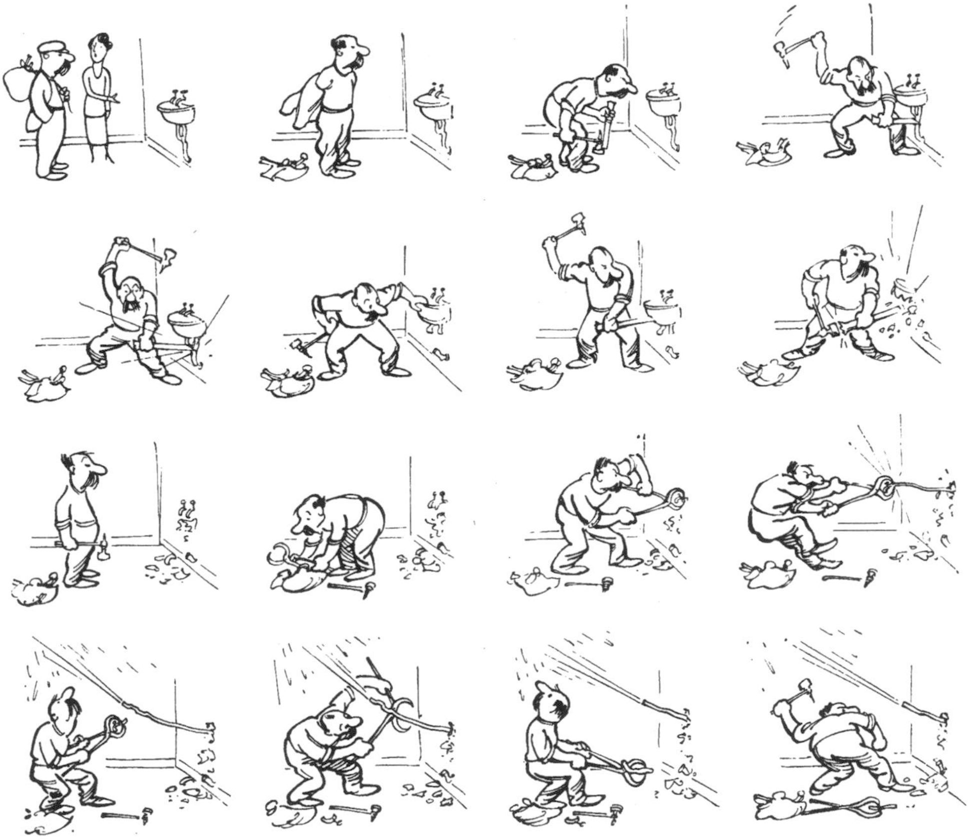

The Plumber

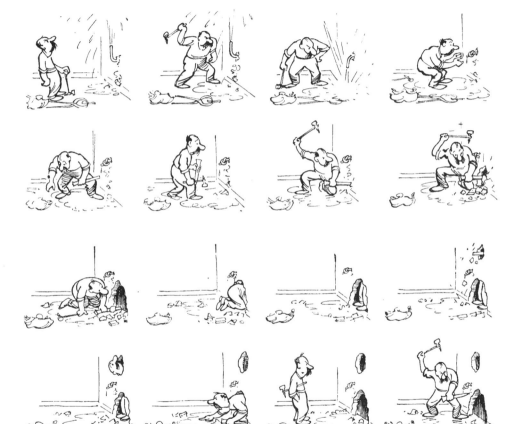

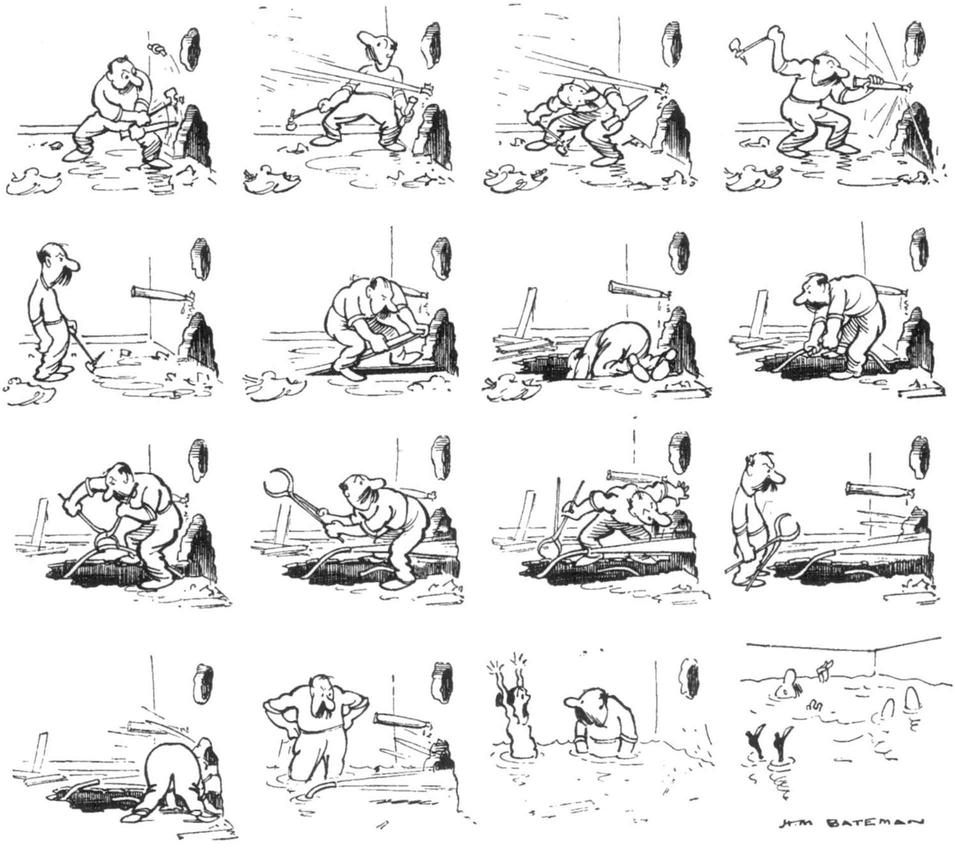
H.M BATEMAN

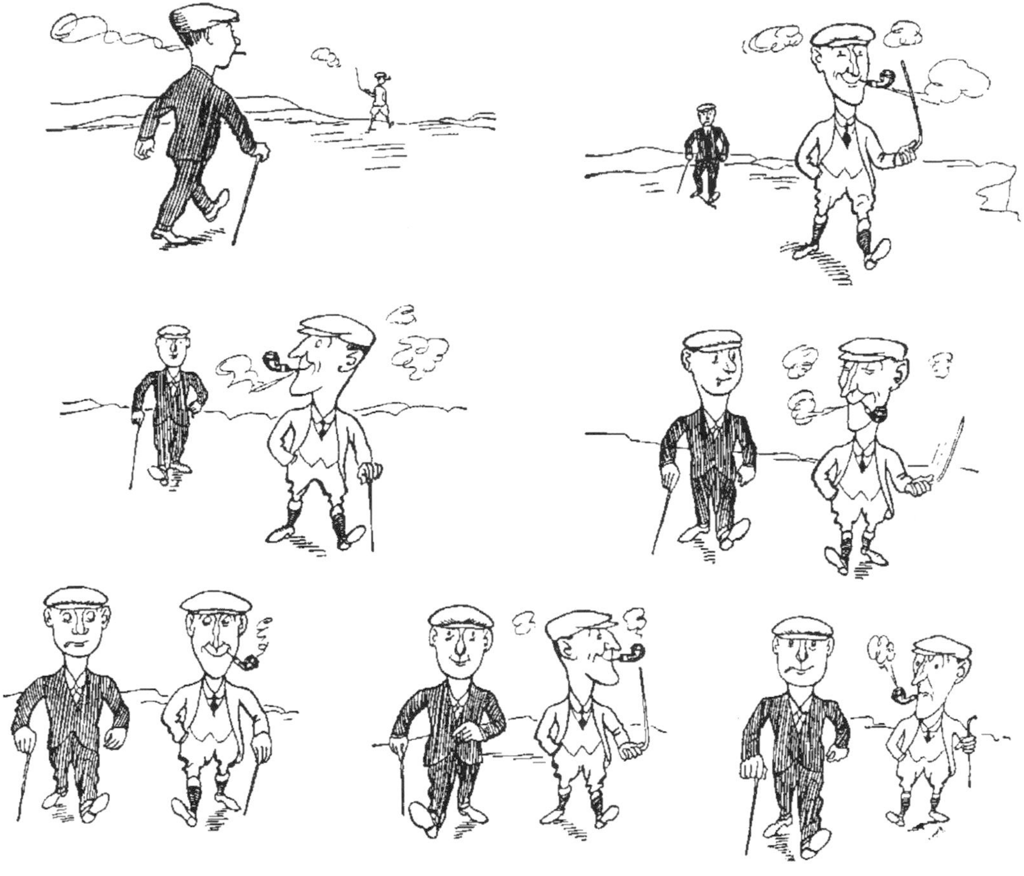

The Walkers

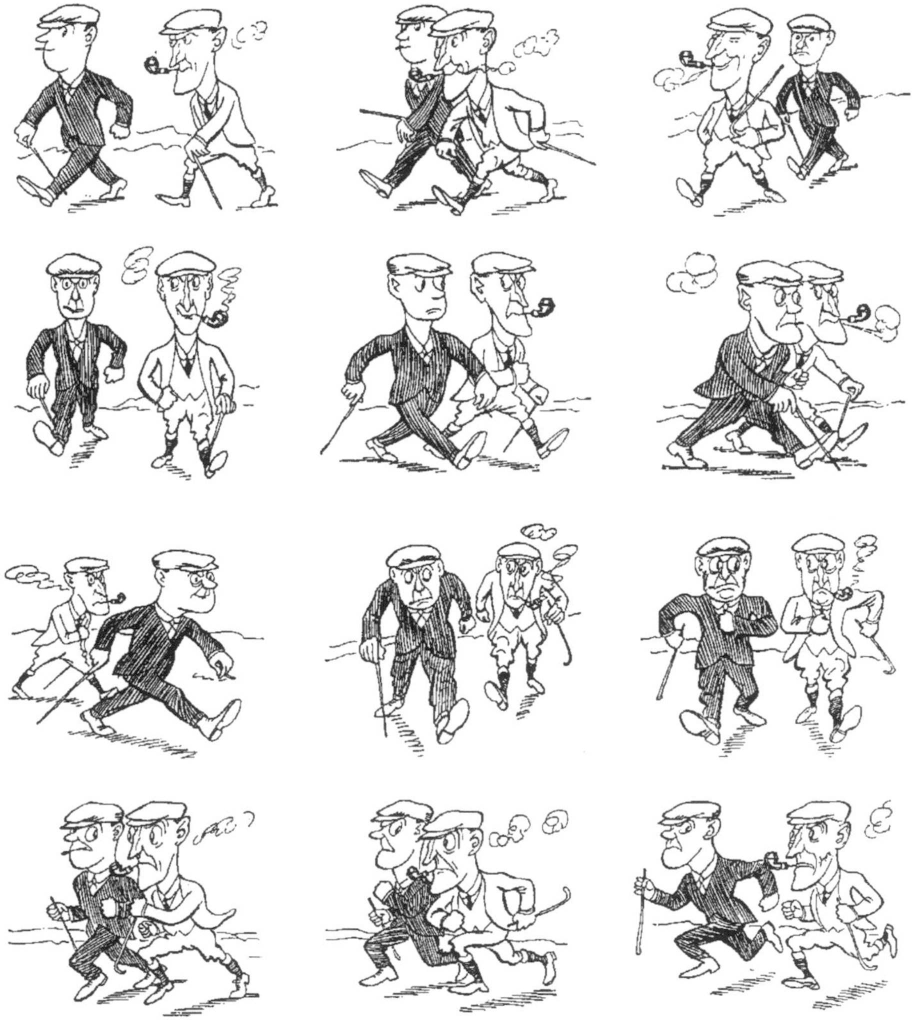

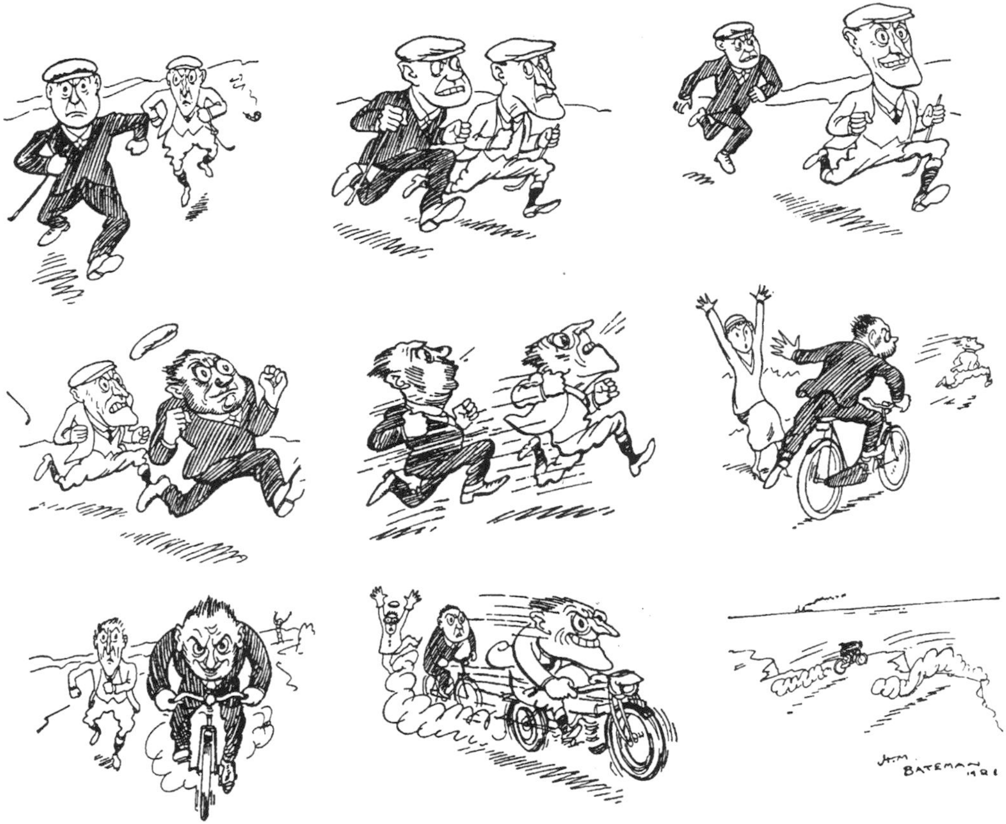
H.M. BATEMAN 1921

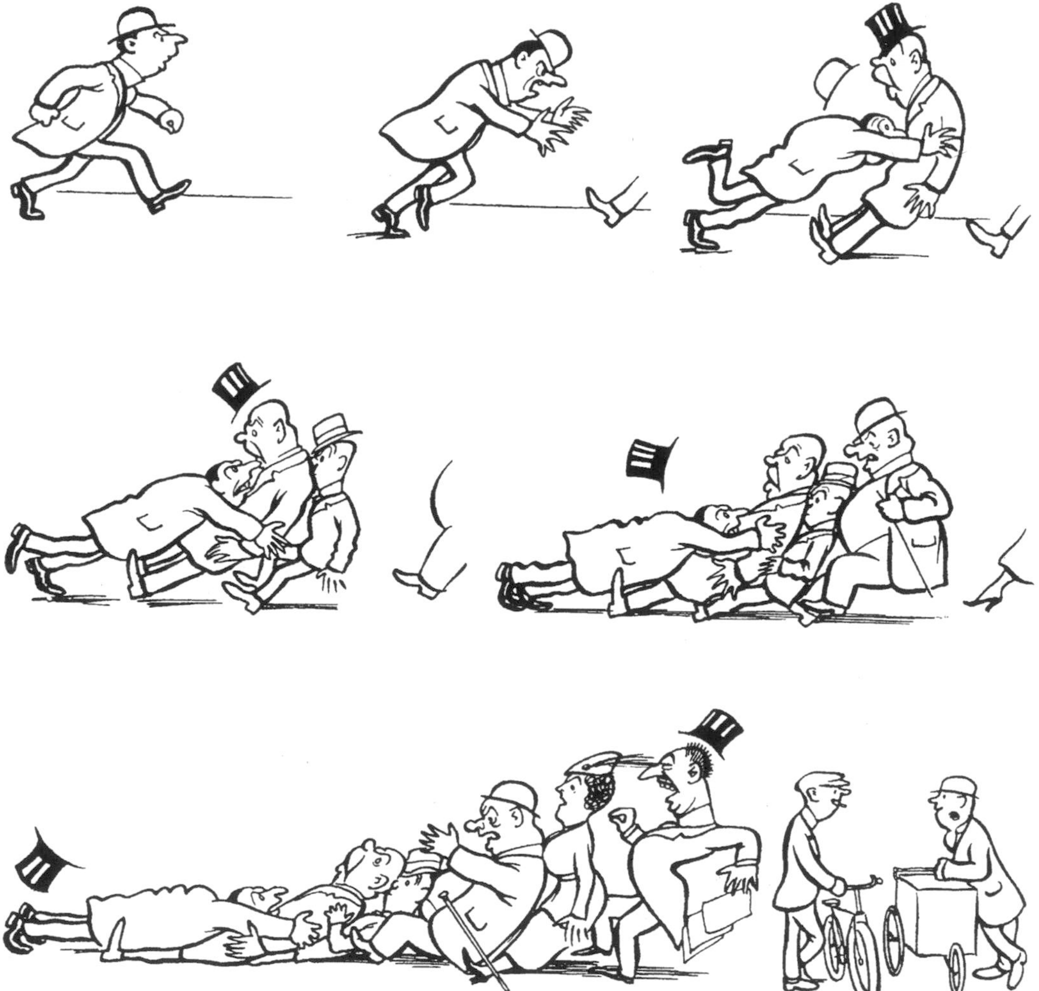

He Slipped

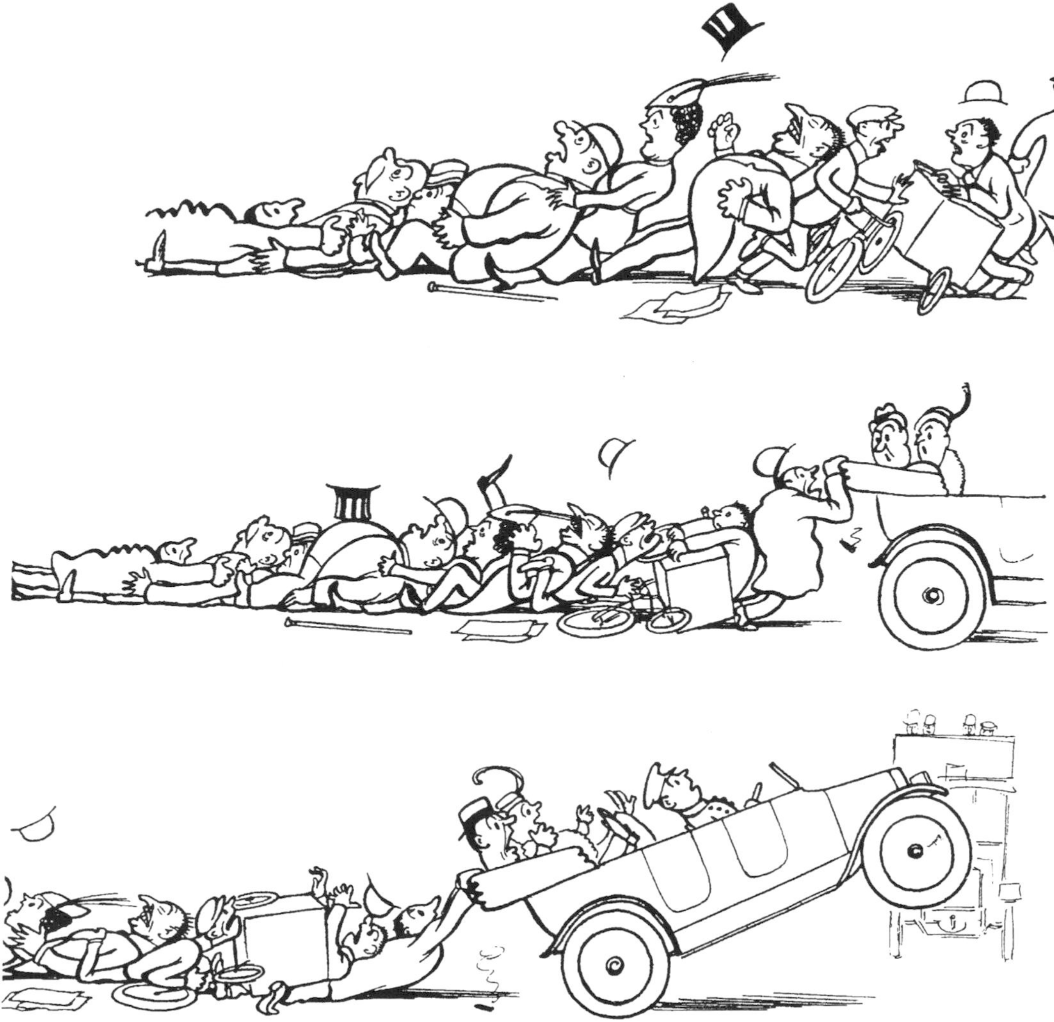

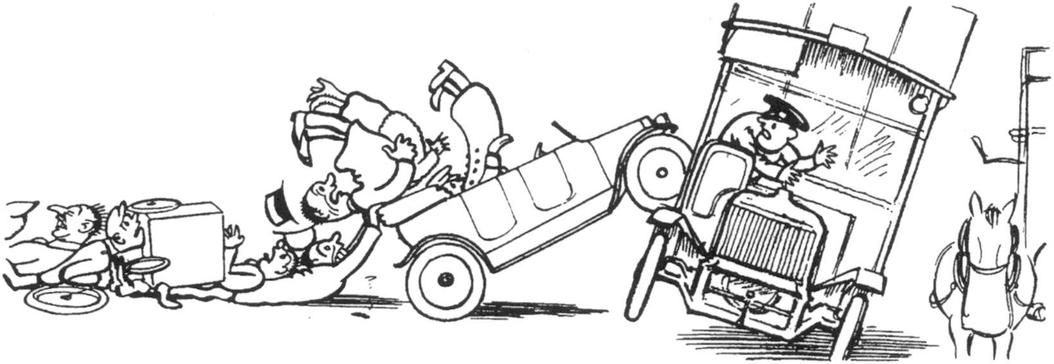

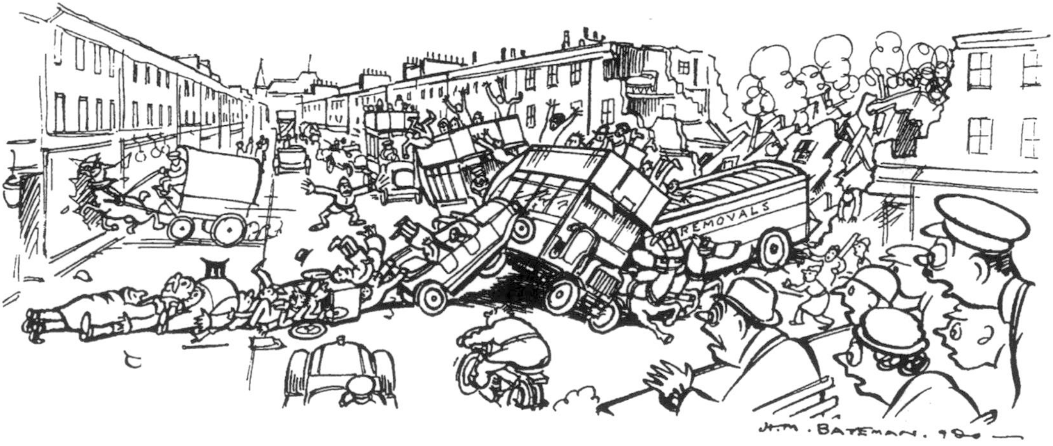
REMOVALS
H.M. BATEMAN

Mark Bryant was born in Dorset and is a philosophy graduate of London University. After a number of years in book publishing – editing acclaimed biographies of the cartoonists Low, Vicky and Searle amongst others – he turned freelance, working as an editor, writer and exhibition curator. Honorary Secretary of the British Cartoonists' Association for eight years (1992–1999), he was also its Vice-President(1999–2000) and is currently Secretary of the London Press Club. He has organized cartoon exhibitions in Poland, Slovakia, Germany, Denmark and France as well as Great Britain, has served on the jury of several international cartoon competitions, and has lectured on the history of cartoons in the UK and overseas. In addition, he is the author of several books – including *Dictionary of British Cartoonists and Caricaturists 1730–1980* (with S. Heneage), *Dictionary of Riddles* (Special Commendation in Best Specialist Reference Book Awards 1990), *Private Lives*, *World War II in Cartoons*, *God in Cartoons* and *Dictionary of 20th Century British Cartoonists & Caricaturists.* He has also edited/compiled more than 20 cartoon collections (amongst other books), including *The Complete Colonel Blimp*, *Vicky's Supermac* and *The Comic Cruikshank*, is a member of the editorial board of the *International Journal of Comic Art*, and has contributed articles on cartoonists and caricaturists to the *New Dictionary of National Biography, Encarta Encyclopedia* and *World Encyclopedia of the Press.*

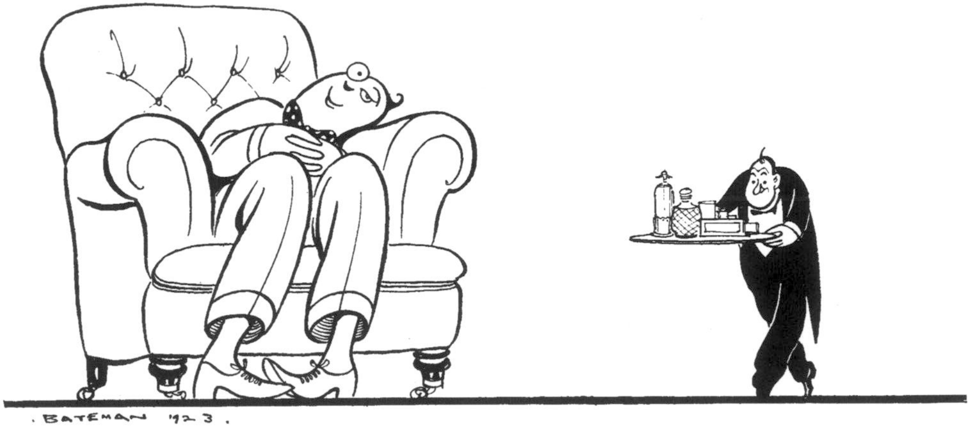
. BATEMAN 1923 .